How to Build the Footy Model PRESTO

How to Build the Footy Model PRESTO

by Flavio Faloci

WoodenBoat BOOKS
Naskeag Road, PO Box 78
Brooklin, Maine 04616 USA
www.woodenboatbooks.com

Published by
WoodenBoat Books
Naskeag Road, PO Box 78
84 Great Cove Drive
Brooklin, Maine 04616 USA
www.woodenboatbooks.com

ISBN 10: 1-934982-06-7
ISBN 13: 978-1-934982-06-8

Photographs by Flavio Faloci
Front Cover photo by Scot Bell

Cover design: BasRelief Design
Text design: Grace Bell

Printed in the USA by Total Printing Systems
10 9 8 7 6 5 4 3 2 1

This book is dedicated to the memory of Angus Richardson, founder of the International Footy Class.

Angus Richardson (left) and Bill Hagerup, at the Liverpool Footy Euro Grand Prix, 2008.

About the Author

Flavio Faloci was born in Rome, Italy in 1965, and resides in Genova (Genoa) not far from the house of Christopher Columbus. His life-long connection with the sea began several generations ago. His grandfather was a tall ship captain and ship owner, as were several generations before his grandfather. Flavio began sailing Optis and building models by age ten. He is a sailing instructor for dinghies and cruising keelboats with the Centor Velico Caprera, the largest sailing/seamanship school in the Mediterranean. Flavio has worked as a yacht surveyor, yacht designer, and is currently employed as a naval architect at the head office of the Registro Italiano Navale, which is the Italian equivalent of the American Bureau of Ships (ABS). He has also been team captain and chief designer of the Trieste Waterbike Team, current holder of the Guinness record for longest distance covered in 24 hours. Other accomplishments include working as an illustrator, the Italian registrar for the Footy model class, and skilled cook of cakes, ice creams, and cookies.

Flavio Faloci, sailing between Corsica and Sardinia

Foreword

At only 12 inches long, Footys are the world's smallest sanctioned radio control model yachts. But don't let the diminutive size fool you—these cute little boats are serious. They perform amazingly well for their size and can be sailed in just about any wind conditions. They can be easily transported when fully rigged, and they can be sailed on small ponds—even in your swimming pool!

The Footy Class was conceived in 2000 by Richard Webb for sailing in small demo pools. A few years later, Footys got more exposure when Brett McCormack published plans for *Bobabout* in New Zealand. One day in 2004, a friend of mine brought a *Bobabout* to our pond that was cute, but didn't sail very well. I thought, "I can make that work," and my own passion for Footys was born. Through the internet, Brett, Roger Stollery from the UK, and I collaborated to create a set of rules that became the nucleus of the class. The basic rule is very simple. It is an open or rule where anything not prohibited or restricted is permitted. All but the rig and sails must fit in a measurement box whose inside dimensions are 305 x 305 x 153 millimeters.

The rule intrigued Angus Richardson, who then joined us. His outwardly gruff manner covered a soft heart, and we became fast friends. His unflagging enthusiasm for these little boats, as well as his incessant prodding to get things done, resulted in the International Footy Class Association, and the adoption of the Footy class in 17 countries. Angus is truly the father of Footys. He passed away in April of 2011, and we miss him greatly. Angus organized the first Footy Euro Grand Prix regatta in Birkenhead, UK in 2008. The race set the tone for friendly, fun competition that remains an important characteristic of the class today. I was fortunate to attend, and made several new friends. Key among those friends was Flavio Faloci, whose understanding of boat design and impeccable construction techniques are second to none.

Footys are lots of fun to build, and wooden construction is a great approach. I've devoted my Footy career to designing simple boats that can be constructed on the kitchen table (with permission from the kitchen owner, of course) with a few simple tools. Despite their simplicity, though, wooden boat designs have been highly competitive in Footy racing, including wins in national championship racing.

While my own designs are racing boats through and through, they don't come close to the beauty and charm of Flavio's creations. Flavio's boats tend toward semi-scale jewels that reflect the heritage of Italian working boats. While not designed specifically for racing, they are good performers that handle great and can be fast, too. And they are so pretty! Flavio is a true artist and craftsman in the old-school tradition. In this book, he shares his design and construction techniques so that you, too, can build and sail an Italian gem. You'll have the prettiest boat on the pond.

— Bill Hagerup
Moultonboro, New Hampshire

Table of Contents

Introduction

Looking to the clouds on the plane returning back home from my entry to the First European Footy Championship in Liverpool (also known as Footy Euro Grand Prix), I was dreaming about a new wooden classical "cruising" Footy.

I was eager to immediately take advantage of the lessons learned during this unforgettable event which was organized by Angus Richardson—the Footy guru—and the friendly Birkenhead Model Yacht Club.

I started to draw a lot of freehand sketches during long, boring, office phone calls, but without a real objective at hand. My laziness prevailed, and all these scrap pieces of paper weren't finalized into an actual new model project.

Only few months later in the fall of 2008, the British Model Yacht Association (MYA) organized a new edition of the Chris Dick Footy Design Award. It was to be an award to the designer(s) of the best new UK Footy Class design of 2008.

Rules were not very strict, leaving me a lot of freedom: "...consideration of hull, foils/bulb and rig/sails will be made using each of the following criteria: shape, innovation and ease of building... designs may be for radio or free sailing, and can be presented in any way that shows the shape and general arrangement of the boat...."

I was kindly invited to enter the contest, even though—at the same time—I was also informed my entry would be automatically disqualified, due to the fact that I wasn't a loyal citizen of the United Kingdom. I was, and I am still, Italian.

Fig 1 Freehand concept "cartoon"

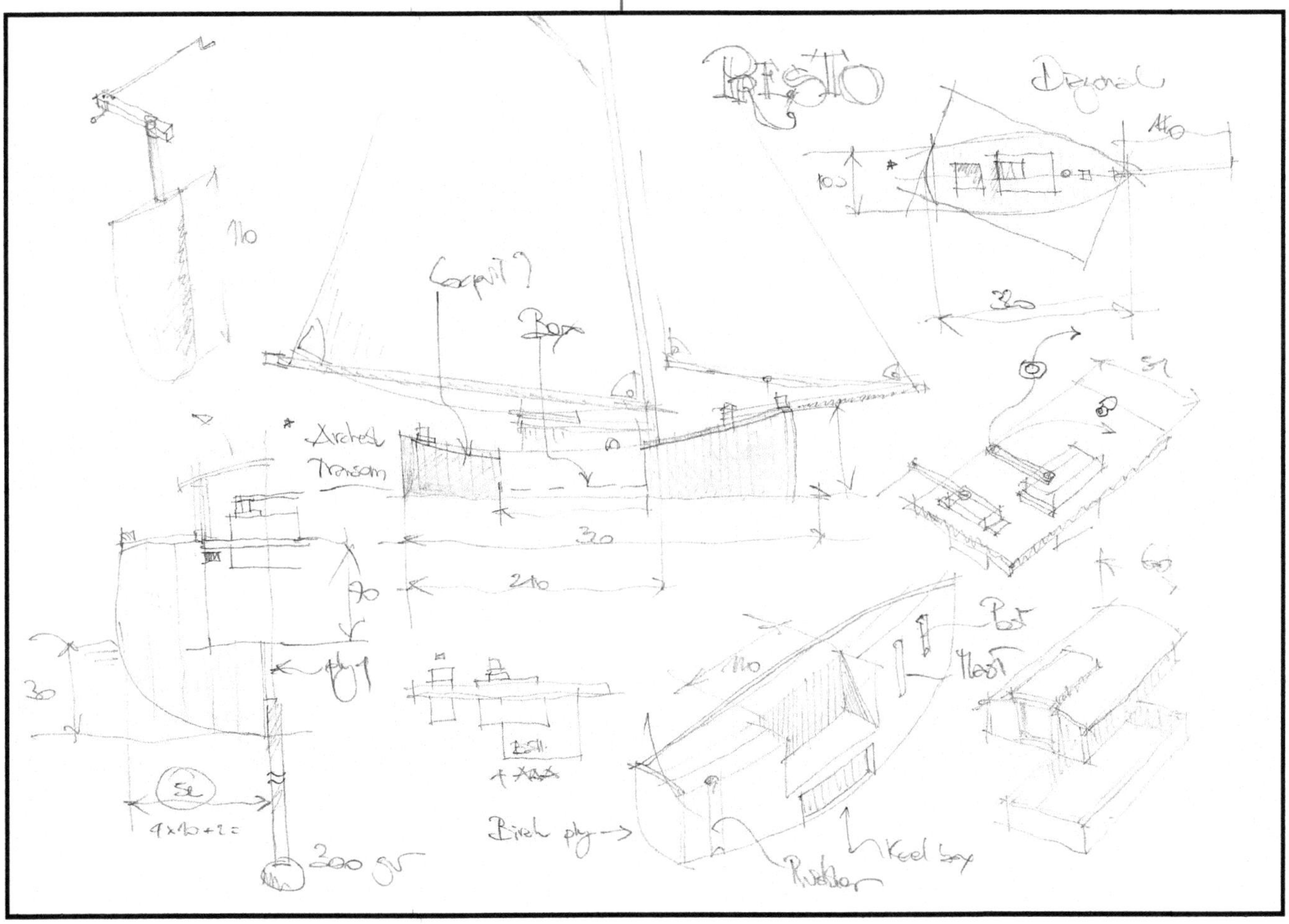

In the meantime, showing a perfect example of gentlemanly sportsmanship, my good friend Roger Stollery (well-known model yacht designer), self-disqualified himself for the lack of legality of his double position of Award Judge, and at the same time, a competition participant. There wasn't a prize, trophy, or money. British are so funny. Without a silver cup, a model race around the buoys, or a real design brief, the only valuable asset of the event for me was a sharp deadline: midnight Friday 14, November 2008. Deadlines, you know, are for lazy modelers. They seem to be the only working means to nail-down uncertain clouds of vague concepts, infinite design options, and never ending project optimizations. Under the pressure of the competition I was able to finalize, at least, a concept design of a basic layout, a sail plan, and preliminary calculations. This is the sail plan I submitted to MYA.

Fig 2 Preliminary sail plan

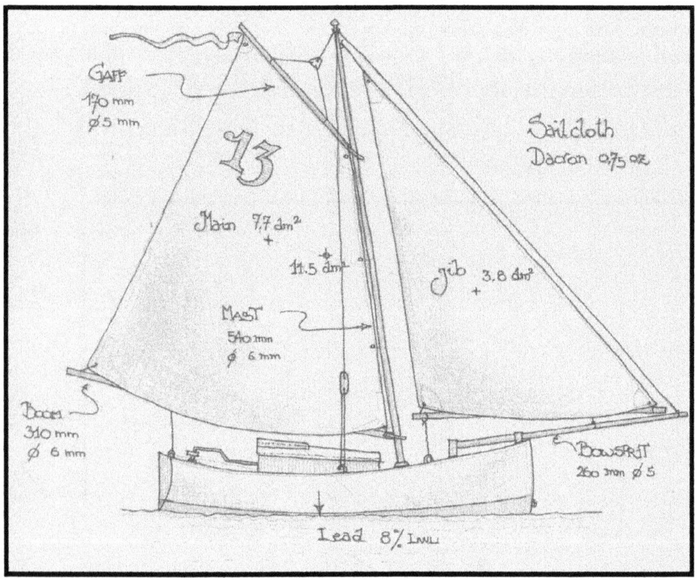

My goal at that time was just a cruising Footy that was pretty, simple, and classical. As far as I know, nobody else was disqualified, and many interesting entries blessed the award. I was fortunate enough to receive several encouraging comments about my drawings. And just few months later, *Presto* started to evolve into a miniature Victorian racing machine.

I started to build the prototype, and didn't resist to add several details aimed to improve her performance, to have a new and competitive boat ready for the second edition of the Footy Euro Grand Prix.

Today, a few years and three sailing prototypes later, the mission profile of this Footy has been explored, ranging from a pure toy boat, to a race winner. Several rigs, keels, and rudders have been tested, and different displacement and sail options have been extensively investigated to improve her performance, and to have a bit of fun.

Design Brief

Model yachts, like their real sisters are designed—or should be designed—to fulfill an ideal wish list, describing the intended goals to be met. Basically, my target was a model designed to fill the gap between extreme racing models (delicate, expensive, and complicated) and ugly beach toys.

Fine tuning the concept "owner's requests" for this Footy were:

- wooden hull (of course!)
- building method aimed to first time builders
- removable electronic components
- easy conversion to/from free-sailer version
- outstanding strength to withstand hard use
- unsinkable
- nice, classic, semi-scale appearance
- decent sailing performance
- scientific engineering optimization of design details

Basic Layout

Main features of the model which were decided during initial step of design process were:

- round bilge hull
- transom stern
- gaff sloop rig
- spade rudder
- fin bulb keel
- semi-scale deckhouse

Sketching several freehand cartoons, a pretty side view of a boat having a "Spirit of Tradition" look began to emerge from my pencil. It was to be a boat with a classic silhouette above water, and modern hull and appendages, but without specific reference to an existing yacht type. Basic three dimensional perspective drawings soon followed, to refine the hull arrangement.

Fig 3 Freehand perspective

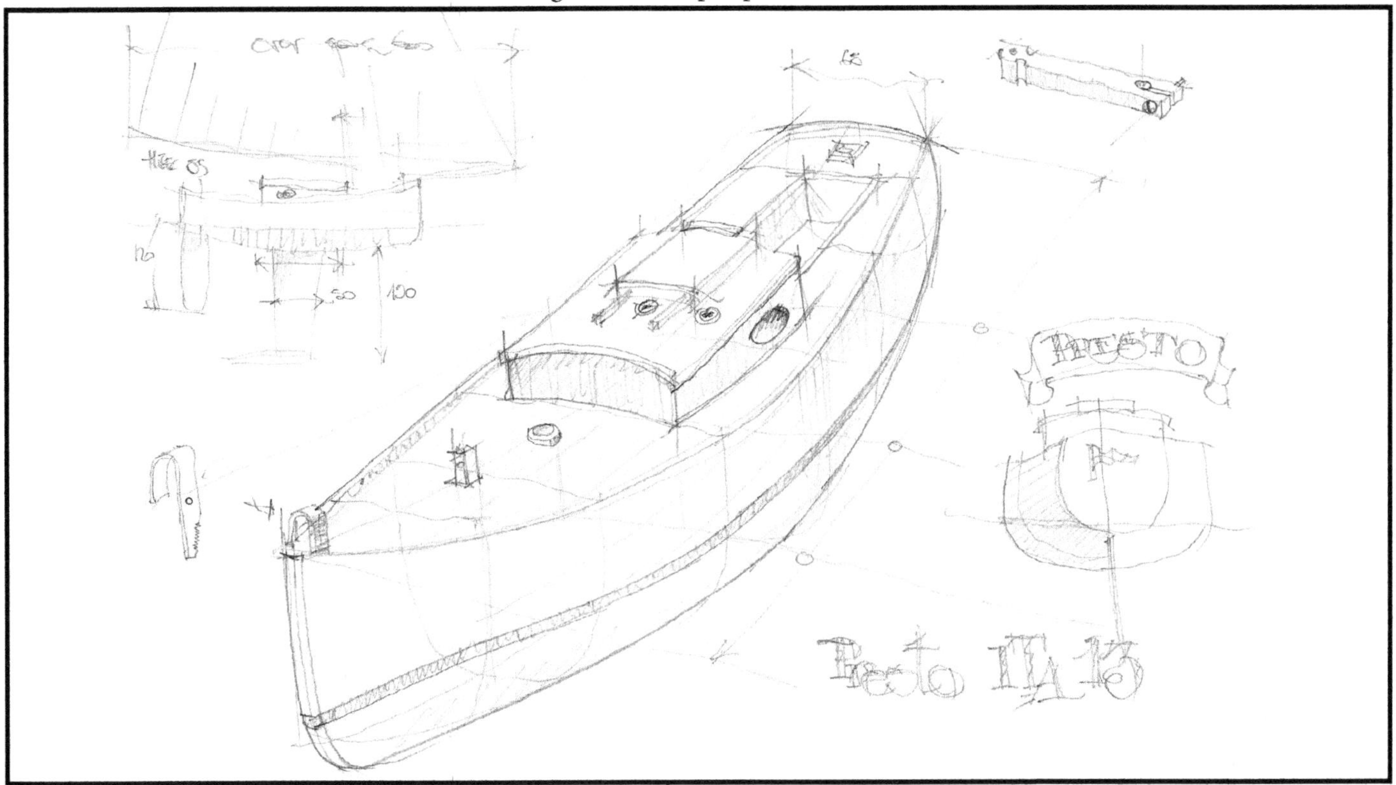

Sail Plan and Rigging

After a first satisfactory definition of model hull, I started to think about the sail plan. *Presto* was conceived from the beginning to be gaff rigged. This choice of an old fashion rig seems to be based just on irrational and emotional reasons (perhaps it is so), but in case of the Footy class, there are good technical reasons to explain this unusual option. Compared to a modern Marconi rig having the same area, a gaff rig has a lower heeling arm, and in turn, a smaller heeling momentum. Under the official Footy Class Rules, sail area is not (yet) measured, so using this gaff rig solution, it's possible to use more canvas for a given amount of hull stability.

Overall, length over spars of *Presto* (from tip of bowsprit to tip of boom) is almost double the length on deck, an eloquent way to explain how sail area is spread lengthwise.

During the 2008 Euro Grand Prix, my first gaff Footy *Folgore* (means lightening thunderbolt in Italian), even with a burned sail servo and sails permanently trimmed for a close reach, did remarkably well arriving fifth overall, ahead of many modern looking competitors.

Angus wrote "Notes on Footy Design Trends" about use of this rig on the International Footy Forum web site:

"This rig gets loads of sail area low down. Centre of effort is low and the rig can generate bags of power. Forget the idea that gaff rigs really will not go to windward. This largely stems from the excessive twist caused by heavy wooden gaffs falling off to leeward, unrestrained by stretchy natural fibre sails."

All spars on board *Presto* are wooden, either tapered and varnished dowels, or four-sided stock which is rounded/tapered as is done on full-scale boats. On my first sail plan I sketched a one piece mast, but when building the prototype I moved to a more classical lower mainmast plus a removable topmast, dreaming of a winter rig arrangement using a smaller jib hoisted on the lower masthead.

Last but not least, this solution is much more transportation friendly if you need to pack your model for an international flight to a remote footy championship abroad.

Running rigging suffered an uncontrolled growth during the building process, and arrived at quite an impressive number of strings to trim:

1. mainsail peak halyard
2. mainsail throat halyard
3. mainsail downhaul
4. mainsail sheet dead end
5. mainsail outhaul
6. jib downhaul
7. jib outhaul
8. jib leech line
9. jib sheet dead end

Not to mention lines for an optional topsail. It's not exactly the number of lines to be expected on a toy boat, but without doubt a nice way to spend a Sunday afternoon on a small pond, searching the ultimate perfect tuning of all these adjustments.

Building Method

Using balsa planks glued on a center plywood keel is a system (also known as bread-and-butter method) that can guarantee a sturdy and watertight hull, even in case of unskilled hands. As a side benefit, we get a good looking and efficient round-bilge hull.

Fig 4 Wonderful beauty of pure wood

Last but not least... cutting, carving, and sanding balsa is a relaxing pleasure for old and young modelers. Drawbacks are the large amount of wasted wood, a lot of sawdust, and a not the lightest of hulls.

Fig 5 Balsa leftover

Angus the Great suggested we build a plank-on-frame lighter and faster version of this hull. Without a doubt she would be much faster, but at the same time, much more complicated to build.

Main Dimensions

After the design concept step, a more detailed feasibility design study was carried out to crunch numbers, looking for a balanced set of key parameters. Broadly speaking, radical designs are usually efficient only within a narrow range of environmental conditions. *Presto* was designed from the beginning to be a quite conservative project (at least from main dimensions point of view), in order to be able to sail under very different wind speeds and wave heights. Following this common sense philosophy, main dimensions have been identified aiming at an efficient all-around project.

-Displacement -
Neither too heavy, nor too light, the initial target mass was established between 500 and 550 grams (approximately 1 to 1¼ pounds) to achieve a proper ballast ratio even with a hull not considered as "feather light". After several sea trials and an extensive tuning-up, I increased overall displacement up to 600 gr, this way using 270 gr of lead, a satisfactory ballast ratio of 45% was achieved. Just to make a comparison, light displacement Footys are a bit less than 350 gr and heaviest models are not far from 1000 gr.

Weight Breakdown

Hull and deckhouse	150 gr
FCU and electric stuff	70 gr
Batteries	40 gr
Spars	30 gr
Sails and rigging	10 gr
Rudder	10 gr
Fin keel	20 gr
Lead ballast	270 gr

- Length -

Following extensive analytical research based on actual naval architecture methods aimed to improve the efficiency of sailing performance, I designed a diagonal hull (fits in the Footy Class Rules 12" x 6" box on the diagonal) as the best compromise between wetted surface and waterline length.

To put it simply, assuming the same displacement and beam, a longer hull has more wetted surface (and more frictional drag), but smaller wave drag in comparison to a shorter version of same boat. Total drag (frictional and wave) is slightly less for shorter hulls at low speed, and a lot less for longer hulls at high speed.

The cross-over for drag vs. speed curves for Footys, is somewhere around one knot. The average Footy sailing speeds are usually between 1.2 and 1.4 knots. For this reason the longer "diagonal" Footys seems to have a definite advantage over shorter "regular" hulls.

Fig 6 Drag curves: long versus short hull comparison

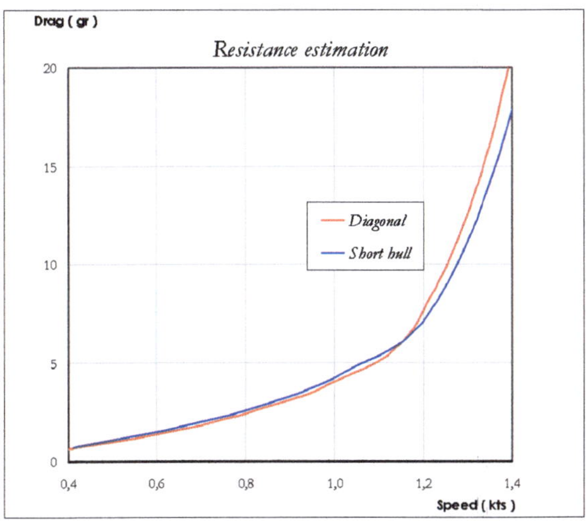

Good performances of this type of Footy hull has been confirmed by outstanding speed of many other racing models, such as Bill Hagerup's *Cobras* and Butch Bragg's *Pool Shark.*

Using a rounded transom stern to take advantage of all available length (rudder not hanging off the transom), I was able to achieve a LWL (loaded waterline length) close to 320 mm, which is approximately 105% of the standard 305 mm Footy length.

Fig 7 Stern transom inside rulebox corner

Doubts about legality of the bowsprit on diagonal hull were raised on an international Footy forum as soon as I disclosed details of this model, but the Footy Technical Committee was kind enough to confirm—on short notice—my point of view, following a request for rule interpretation.

-Beam-

Breadth was established as a harmonized compromise between drag and stability requirements, as well taking into account the building method, the keel thickness, plus an even number of wood planks. Final beam is 100 mm, much below the allowed 150 mm maximum. Waterline beam is almost the same of maximum hull beam.

-Depth-

Hull height has been dictated by the need to house an inner hold big enough to fit the remote control set if needed, and to have a satisfactory midship freeboard to achieve a large "deck awash" heel angle.

-Sail Area-
The first sail plan was drawn following the well established procedure "if it looks right it should be right". During a following design step, rig size has been optimized based on stability calculations, aiming at a 30° heel angle at 10-12 knots of true wind speed. Standard rig size is 12.3 dm2 (square decimeters, approximately 190 square inches). To suit changes of wind speed, I have also tested both mainsail reefing, and an additional topsail.

Fig 8 Heel angle vs. wind speed

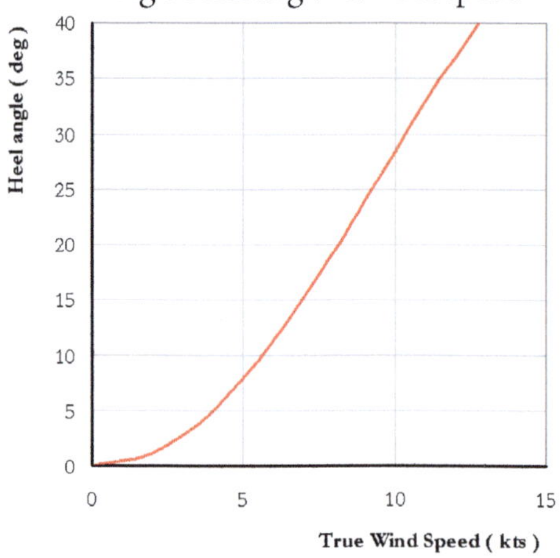

-Appendages Size -
Maximum fin span has been dictated by the rules allowed for vertical distance between the bottom of the ballast bulb, and top of the hull (305 mm).

Keel chord has been adjusted to meet an initial target side area around 8% of sail area. Following additional hydrodynamic research, this coefficient has been increased up to 11%, with pleasant windward performance improvements. (Keel chord is the distance between the leading edge and trailing edges of the keel, measured mid-way down the keel.)

Keel side shape is slightly trapezoidal in order to reduce heeling arm, moving the center of effort up, and to improve stiffness of the fin blade.

Keel thickness has been tested using both 4mm and 2mm plywood. The first rudder area was 60% of the keel, but after the first races, blade area has been reduced, with a small speed gain, and without affecting smart manoeuvring performance.

Remote Control Inners

Following a first estimate of hull depth and beam, I started to think how to stuff my *Presto* with small expensive electric gear. I like to mount all electronic components (rudder and sail servos, batteries, switch, receiver) on a small removable plank for the FCU (Footy control unit). Using this arrangement, it is much easier to repair, modify, adjust, or remove the small wonder boxes that make the miracle of remote control possible. The system seems to work, and I now use it on all my new models.

Fig 9 Plywood FCU

On first version of *Presto*, I envisaged the use of 4 AA batteries in accordance to old Footy rule requirements. But on following versions, the size of the FCU was reduced, taking advantage of reduced size (and weight) of 4 AAA batteries. Use of even smaller and lighter Ni Cad rechargeable batteries, if you wish, is possible and advisable.

Use of hi-tech LiPo ultralight batteries, due to their noisy and bad habit of exploding when short circuited, is not recommended. These wonderful things are wonderful when far from water, but Footy gaskets can leak, so why risk it?

Servo torque has been assessed to be on the safe side, after having witnessed the cruel death of screaming gears, and the silent burning failures of electronic parts of not less than a dozen of these devices. I have destroyed three of them on my own, and I am now a worldwide renowned expert on the topic.

Geometry of sail servo arrangement: the servo position and arm length, fairleads holes position and sheets, connection to jib and mainsail boom, may look a bit chaotic, but they have been carefully studied to achieve a satisfactory set-up, aimed to have an automatically independent trim of mainsail and jib sheeting angles. This geometry enables fine adjustment of jib sheeting angle, while the main remains more or less constant at close-hauled. I used this trick to ease the jib sheet before tacks. Footys are sometimes a bit lazy, and in case of waves, there are remarkable possibilities to miss a few tacks. It should be noted that on bigger models, a reverse set-up is typically used to "dump the main" in puffs, while keeping the jib in, to keep the boat from rounding up.

Based on the size and position of rudder and sail servos, as well as their arm geometry, I sketched a first configuration of a feasible FCU. Required length, breadth, and height of the FCU were estimated, sketching an ideal brick having extreme dimensions of this box.

Hull Shape

Hull shape was designed having an "internal" design constraint of the remote control box, and as external limits, the rulebox boundaries.

Longitudinal position of the hold, designed to house inner electronics, was established keeping in mind the mast position as a forward limit, as well a proper location of center of gravity of this heavy cargo.

Hull surface was designed to wrap an ideal brick having extreme dimensions of the FCU. Even if I like an initial paper and pencil approach, help of three dimensional design software has been, in this case, very useful. After several trials and errors, I have been able to design an efficient and fair underwater shape, leaving enough "meat" between inner box corners and hull bottom.

Fig 10 Hull surface and internal box

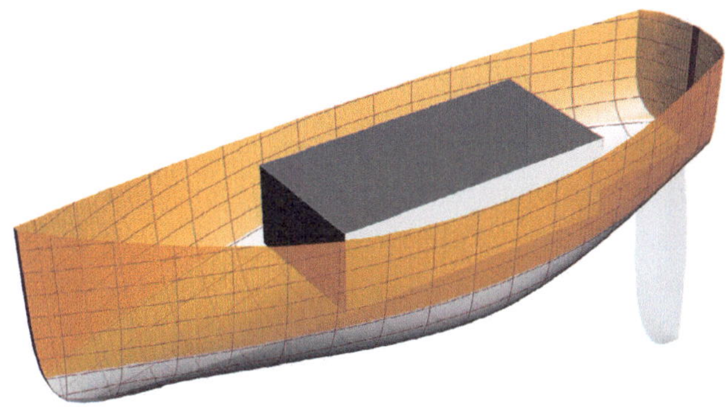

Bow entrance angle, as well stern transom shape were drawn to be tangent to the box's sides.

Fig 11 Bow detail inside rulebox corner

A nice sheerline was designed to achieve plenty of bow freeboard in order to avoid nose-diving problems, one of the most discussed features of Footy design.

Longitudinal center of buoyancy and prismatic coefficient were decided, having a high relative speed sailing in mind. A gentle breeze, from a Footy point of view, is a strong wind, and for this simple reason these hulls are usually sailing at quite high relative speeds. In many cases they approach hull speed even when going to windward.

A slightly immersed transom was also a small design detail introduced to improve high speed running. By the way, in this case "high speed" means something not exceeding 1.5 knots!

Hull Balance

The fin keel has been designed to be housed within a slot on hull bottom. Its position has been dictated by wanting a perfectly even keel/longitudinal floating trim.

Having preliminary hull and appendages almost defined, I started to draw the sail plan. Keeping the mast position and rake fixed, I adjusted its length as well as bowsprit and boom lengths to meet the sail area requirements, and a balanced longitudinal position of the center of effort. Lead between the sail plan and lateral plane is approximately 9% of LWL (loaded waterline length). The geometric center of the sail plan is not far from one quarter chord of the fin keel.

To speed up the work, I used several semi-complicated excel spreadsheets I created to streamline this and other design calculations. Thanks to a lot of guess work and a bit of pure luck, *Presto* is at the same time very balanced under all points of sail, and also has a quick response to the rudder.

First Prototype – *Presto* MK I –

After several handmade pencil drawings, and a lot of computer printouts, I started to convert wood into sawdust, hoping to be able to build this new Footy fast enough to enter the 2009 edition of Euro Grand Prix.

As usual, the model was finished in my Liverpool hotel room, and she was launched a quarter of hour before the start of the first race. This last minute procedure seems to be quite popular among the yacht modeler community. The first version of *Presto* was built in a hurry using thick balsa planks (five 10 mm layers on each side) hoping to reduce the time needed to build the hull.

Fig 12 *Presto* MKI midship section

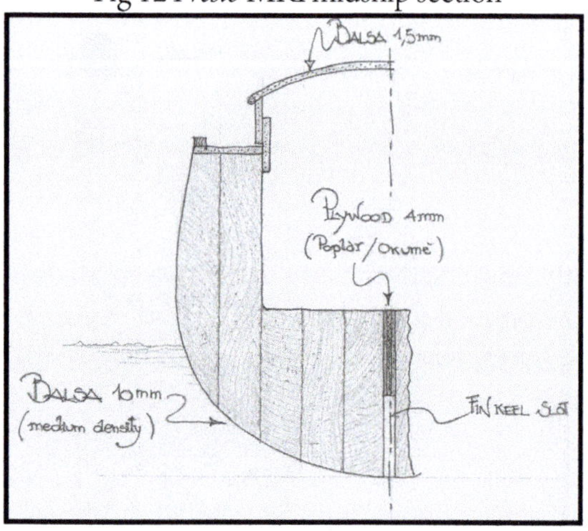

The inner hold was quite large to house a big pack of four AA batteries, so the deckhouse was also quite long—a bit too long from an aesthetic point of view.

Due to the small distance between the transom stern and aft side of the long deckhouse, the aft deck was built flush without a scale cockpit well.

In saving time, I forgot to carefully check mass density of the balsa planks used to build the hull. On completion of the model, using the so called "reverse engineering method" I discovered that, unfortunately, the specific gravity of these planks was close to values usually accustomed for well-seasoned teak. To put it simply, the hull was outrageously heavy. To save more time, I used a heavy recycled ballast bulb, and a standard 4AA pack. In spite of the fact that final displacement was around 850 grams (154 % of estimated planned mass), *Presto* sailed quite well, both under storm rig as well as under the standard rig.

Fig 13 Storm rig

Fig 14 Under standard rig (note the long deck house)

This time my sail servo had broken apart on only the second day of the championship, which was actually a remarkable improvement compared with the immediate failure suffered by my *Folgore,* the previous year.

The exceptional structural strength of the hull, and that she is unsinkable, enabled me to finish all the races arriving with a 6th place overall. Not so bad for a "cruising" Footy.

Fig 15 *Presto* on the green of the Birkenhead Model Yacht Club

Other competitors, under the combined effect of Liverpool oceanic wind and rain, simply disappeared (above or below the water).

Back home, *Presto* underwent an extensive upgrade: the electronic block size was reduced, FCU was rearranged, I made use of a smaller AAA battery pack, and a smaller (and prettier) deckhouse was rebuilt. Also, fin keel shape, size, weight, and position were modified, as well as rudder size and shape adjustments. And, running rigging details were also fine-tuned. All this activity was rewarded with nine "first to finish" out of ten races.

Fig 16 Modified Presto undergoing sea trials

Following my Footy catboat *Brando, Presto* MKI was packed and mailed (after a fresh coat of varnish) to the other side of the pond, to be put on display during the 2010 WoodenBoat Show at the Mystic Seaport Museum in Mystic, Connecticut.

Fig 17 Presto MKI final touch-up

Second Prototype – British *Presto* –

My good friend Andrew Halstead, a smart British engineer and modeler with a very open mind, was interested in both radical design solutions, as well to more classical boats, like my designs. He even designed and built a sailing Viking ship, a square-rigged Footy.

During the development of my first version of *Presto* he asked me to introduce a pair of small modifications to suit his taste.

First of all, he did not want a diagonal measured Footy. Instead, he wanted a transom hung rudder instead of my spade version. His second requirement was a rearrangement of longitudinal sections to enable him to use a greater number of thinner lift planks.

Fig 18 Andrew's *Presto* version

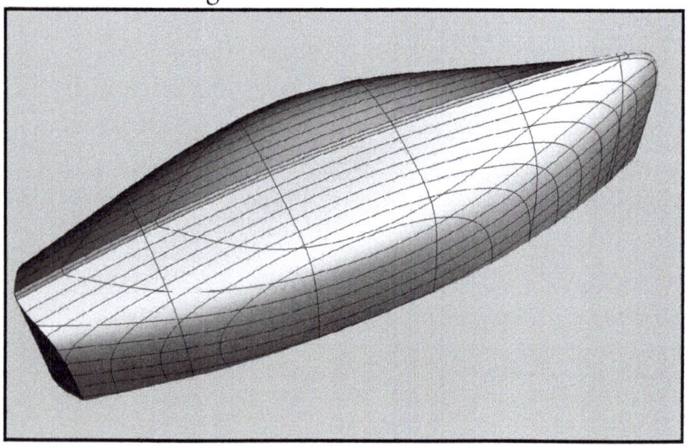

He used eight + eight 6 mm (1/4") planks, instead of my five + five 10 mm (3/8").

Thinner planks means a greater number of parts to cut, but thinner planks can be cut faster using a blade knife instead of a jigsaw. More planks means more time-consuming work with glue to connect all the bread-and-butter parts, but at the same time, it's simpler and faster for shaping work. All considered, Andrew's option was the best compromise, and I adopted it for my second prototype of *Presto*.

Fig 19 Five planks each side

Fig 20 Eight planks each side

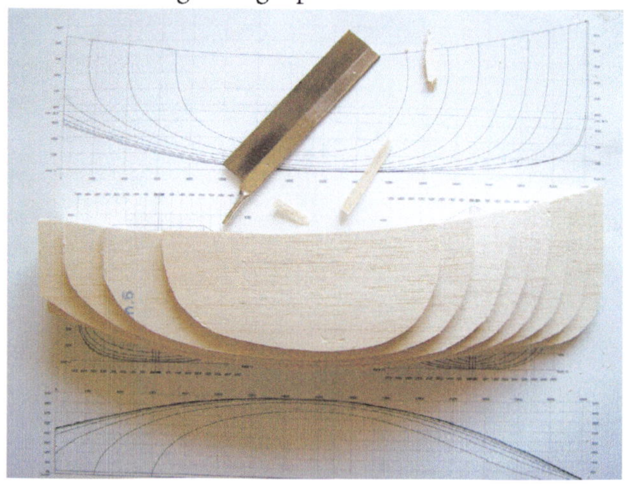

Once again the thin planks option was considered the most suitable building method, when also taking into account the cost of materials.

Andrew and I decided to take part in the 2009 edition of the Footy EuroGrand Prix, as a gaffer team named "Scuderia Presto". (Editor's note: Scuderia means "stable" and is typcially used with racing teams, *Scuderia Ferrari,* for example. Flavio is a competitor.)

Fig 21 Scuderia Presto going to windward

Andrew asked me to register his Footy under Italian Flag, due to the fact that he is a proud owner of a Ducati motorcycle, and because he spent his honeymoon in Venice. His *Presto* was launched just one or two days before the event, sporting a nice bright red suit of sails, in fishing boat fashion, and registered as ITA 22. Material for his sail was provided by a recycled umbrella. Due to a lack of time to fine tune our Footys we didn't win the Team Trophy, but we enjoyed a fun event.

Third Prototype – *Presto* MK II –

Due to the fact that my first *Presto* was visiting Maine, and that the 2010 edition of Euro Grand Prix was scheduled in Poland in July, in just two weeks, I hurridly built a new refined version of this Footy.

Building a second, almost sistership model enabled me to introduce several improvements, and at the same time, adjust many details taking advantage of the lessons learned during races and sea trials. One change was adding a small cockpit well to improve her semi-scale look, as well to save a bit of weight.

Fig 22 *Presto* MK II

Hull shape was slighty modified introducing subtle changes to the bow. I "filled" the waterline hollow entrance, to simplify building (concave surfaces are more difficult to carve than convex) and to have a slight increase of prismatic coefficient. Note the differences between upper right corners of Fig 17 and Fig 22.

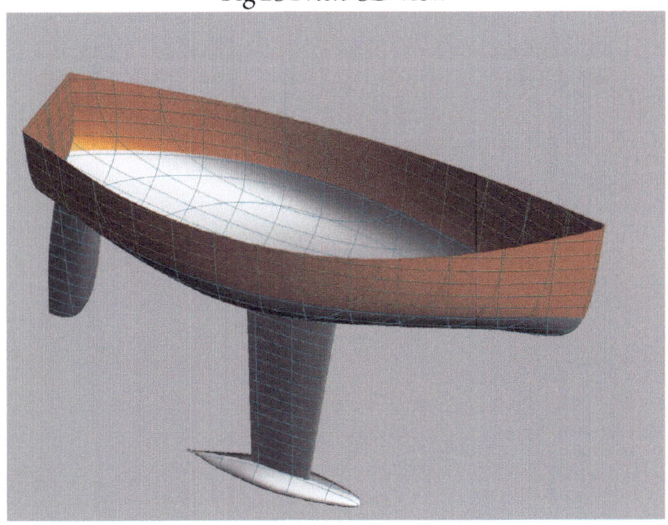

Fig 23 *Presto* 3D view

Even though I have not been able to organize a match race between the two versions, it has been very interesting to analyze different shapes of bow waves on these two models. See Fig 24 and Fig 25.

Fig 24 Wave shape on first *Presto* at hull speed

Fig 25 Waves on second *Presto*

Rigging details were optimized and adjusted to simplify handling of the running rigging "spaghetti".

A third version of the FCU was designed and built to save weight and space.

And, last but not least, a careful monitoring of balsa density was carried out before building, enabling me to save a remarkable amount of hull weight.

Wood weight, converted in lead weight, was shifted to the bulb, lowering the center of gravity of the model, and in turn improving her stability.

Once again, notwithstanding a last minute launch in a beautiful Polish lake, my *Presto* sailed remarkably well, arriving in sixth place on a fleet of approximately 30 modern looking Footys, many of them sporting black carbon-fiber hulls.

Experience gained during the building of these models, and a detailed record of building operations, have been the basis for this book and a wonderful way to share my fun with other modelers around the world.

—Flavio Faloci
Genova, Italy

Fig 26 Racing in Wroclaw, Poland

Tools, Materials, Suppliers

TOOLS
Razor (x-acto type) knife
Jigsaw or coping saw
Steel rule
Clothes pins for clamping
Headed straight pins
C-clamps
Pliers / wire cutters
Scissors
Pencil
Wood rasp
Sand paper, various grades
Small files
Small hand drill

MATERIALS
Balsa planks, thickness 3/32" (2 mm): Deck and deckhouse
Balsa planks, thickness ¼" (6 mm): Hull lifts
Balsa stringers, sides 3/32" x 3/32" (2 mm x 2 mm): Toe rail
Plywood (liteply, poplar, okumè), thickness 1/8"-5/32" (3-4 mm): Fin keel and rudder blade, RC tray
Plywood (birch), thickness 1/16" (1.5 mm): Spar jaws, bowsies
Plywood (birch), thickness 1/32" (0.8 mm): Stern transom, nameplate
Plywood (birch), thickness 3/16" (5 mm): Mast caps
Hardwood (mahogany, walnut), sides 3/16" x 3/16" (5 mm x 5 mm): Sampson post, tiller
Dowels (medium density wood) or square spruce stock for spars (note: standard birch dowels may be too dense/heavy)
Diameter 3/16" (5 mm): Topmast and gaff
Diameter ¼" (6 mm): Mainmast, boom, bowsprit, rudderstock

MATERIALS, con't.
Medium density wood (fir, ash, lime, samba, spruce) strips, sides 3/32" x ¼" (2 mm x 6 mm): Jib boom, three laminated strips
Ballast lead: Fishing sinker, approximate weight 9-10 oz (250-300 gr)
Nail: 1/2" long for attaching keel bulb to keel
Small screw: Approximately 3/8" long, for tiller
Two clips (either fishing or jewelry): Attaching main sheet and jib sheets to booms
Three wooden or plastic beads: Trim pieces for cabin top and sail servo, can be made from scrap wood
Sail cloth: Light Dacron, ¾ - 1 oz/sq yd (40–50 gr /dm^2)
Dacron sail tape for sail reinforcements
Brass Rod 1/16" and 1/32" diameter: deck fittings, rigging, nameplate nails
Cardboard (not corrugated) for hull patterns
Clear Plastic for portholes
Dacron braided fishing line: 20 lb test, for rigging, approximately 15'
Pennant
Radio Control, specs per plans page 9
Paint, varnish as desired
Cyano glues: Super Glue, Crazy Glue
Aliphatic glues: Carpenter's Wood Glue, Titebond, Titebond III

SUPPLIERS
Local hobby shops may be your best resource for all materials needed. Here are a few specific suppliers:

Radio Control:
www.towerhobbies.com (US)
www.radioyachtsuppliesaustralia.com (Australia)
www.wonderlandmodels.com (UK)

Wood:
www.nationalbalsa.com (US)
www.balsausa.com (US)
www.alwayshobbies.com (UK)
www.hobbyco.com.au (Australia)

Sailcloth:
www.sailrite.com (US)
www.pjsails.co.uk (UK)

OTHER USEFUL RESOURCES
Footy Class R/C Sailboats
www.footy.rcsailing.net
Footy Seniors
www.footy-seniors.com
Italian Footy Class Site
www.footy.it
American Model Yacht Association
www.theamya.org/boats/footy
Australian Radio Yachting Association
www.radiosailing.org.au
Canadian Radio Yachting Association
www.crya.ca
Model Yachting Association Great Britain
www.myauk.wordpress.com
NZ Radio Yachting Association
www.nzradioyachtingassociation.co.nz
UK Radio Control Council
www.ukrcc.org

FOOTY CLASS RULES for ***radio*** sailing

Full size insignia

These are **open class rules** in which anything not specifically restricted or prohibited is permitted.

A. GENERAL
A.1 This class is administered by the Footy Class Association. The Footy Class Charter is posted at http://footy.rcsailing.net.charter.php
A.2 The metric dimensions relate to a boat approximately 1 foot long.

B. PRIMARY MEASUREMENT RULE
B.1 With the exceptions listed below in B.2, B.3, B.4 and B.5 the **boat** in racing trim shall be capable of fitting into an open-topped rectangular measurement box of internal dimensions 305mm long, 305mm deep, 153mm wide, with 6.3mm wide slots for projecting **spars** and **rudder,** as shown in the diagram. Racing trim means all components of the **boat** shall be installed and be capable of the full motion used while racing, without being restricted by any part of the measurement box.
B.2 The following may project above the top of the measurement box: **sail(s), mast(s), spars, rigging,** aerial, wind indicator(s), associated fittings.
B.3 A **bowsprit** may project forward of the measurement box.
B.4 The following may project aft of the measurement box: bumpkin, **rudder.**
B.5 During measurement, rotation of a **rudder** extending through the slot is unnecessary.

C. CONDITIONS FOR RACING
C.1 Radio control is restricted to the use of no more than 2 channels.
C.2 Batteries shall be placed within the **hull.**
C.3 During an event, **ballast** shall not be changed, moved or rotated relative to the **hull.**

D. HULL
D.1 The **hull** registration number shall be clearly and legibly marked in an easily visible location either inside or outside on a non-removable part of the **hull(s)** by any of the following means: painting on, engraving in, bonding in, moulding in.

E. HULL APPENDAGES
E.1 The overhang of a **rudder** is restricted to 51mm aft of the measurement box.
E.2 Except for **rudder(s),** the following are prohibited: retractable and or movable **hull appendages.**
E.3 The thickness of a **rudder** extending aft of the measurement box shall not exceed 6.3mm.
E.4 The density of composite materials for ballast shall not exceed that of lead (11300kg/m^3). Composite materials are defined as a mixture of materials brought together to form a single component.

F. RIG
F.1 More than one **bowsprit** is prohibited. The **bowsprit spar cross section** shall fit within a 6.3mm diameter circle.
F.2 More than one bumpkin is prohibited. The bumpkin spar cross section shall fit within a 6.3mm diameter circle.
F.3 Fittings shall be no bigger than is reasonably required for their primary purpose(s).

G. SAIL IDENTIFICATION
G.1 Apply to the Footy Class registrar for registration number.
G.2 The class insignia shall be displayed on both sides of the mainsail as shown in the diagram. They may be handed and placed back to back.
G.3 Sail numbers shall comply with the current ISAF RRS with the following exceptions:
(a) all dimensions shall be divided by 2.
(b) sail numbers shall be displayed on mainsails only and need not comply with E6(e)3.
(c) **boats** with sail numbers 01,08,10,18,80 and 81 shall display a prefix '1', unless the number requires changing at an event due to a conflict.

Please see the website http://www.footy.rcsailing.net for more information

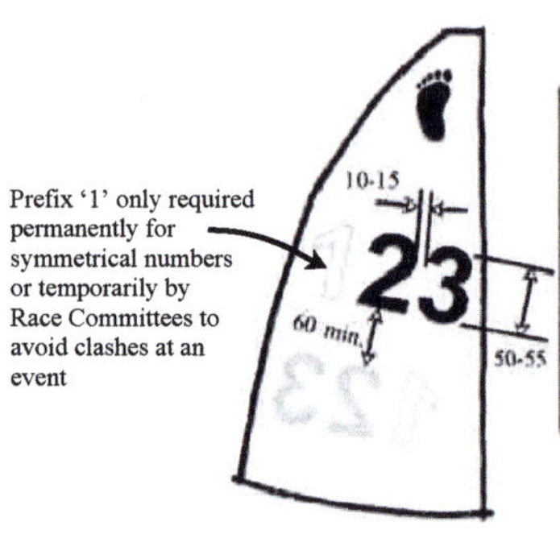

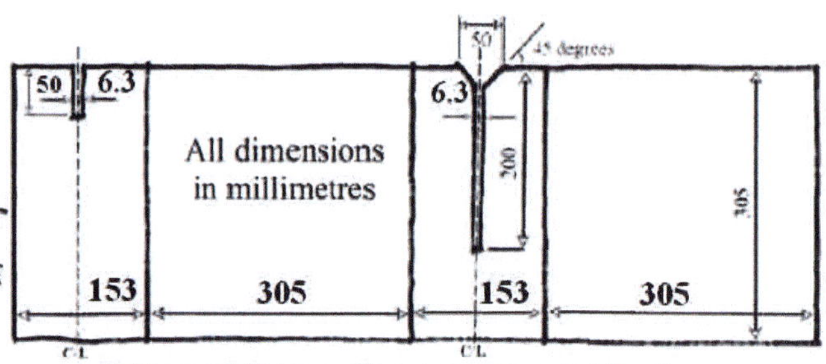

Internal faces of measurement box

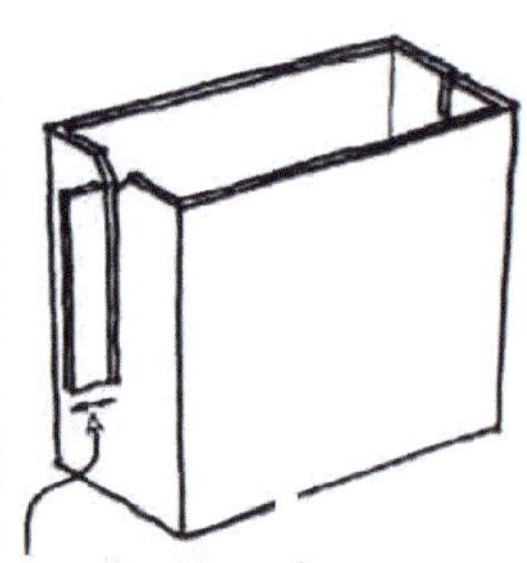

Gauge for **rudder** overhang 51mm from inner face of 'box'

Plans

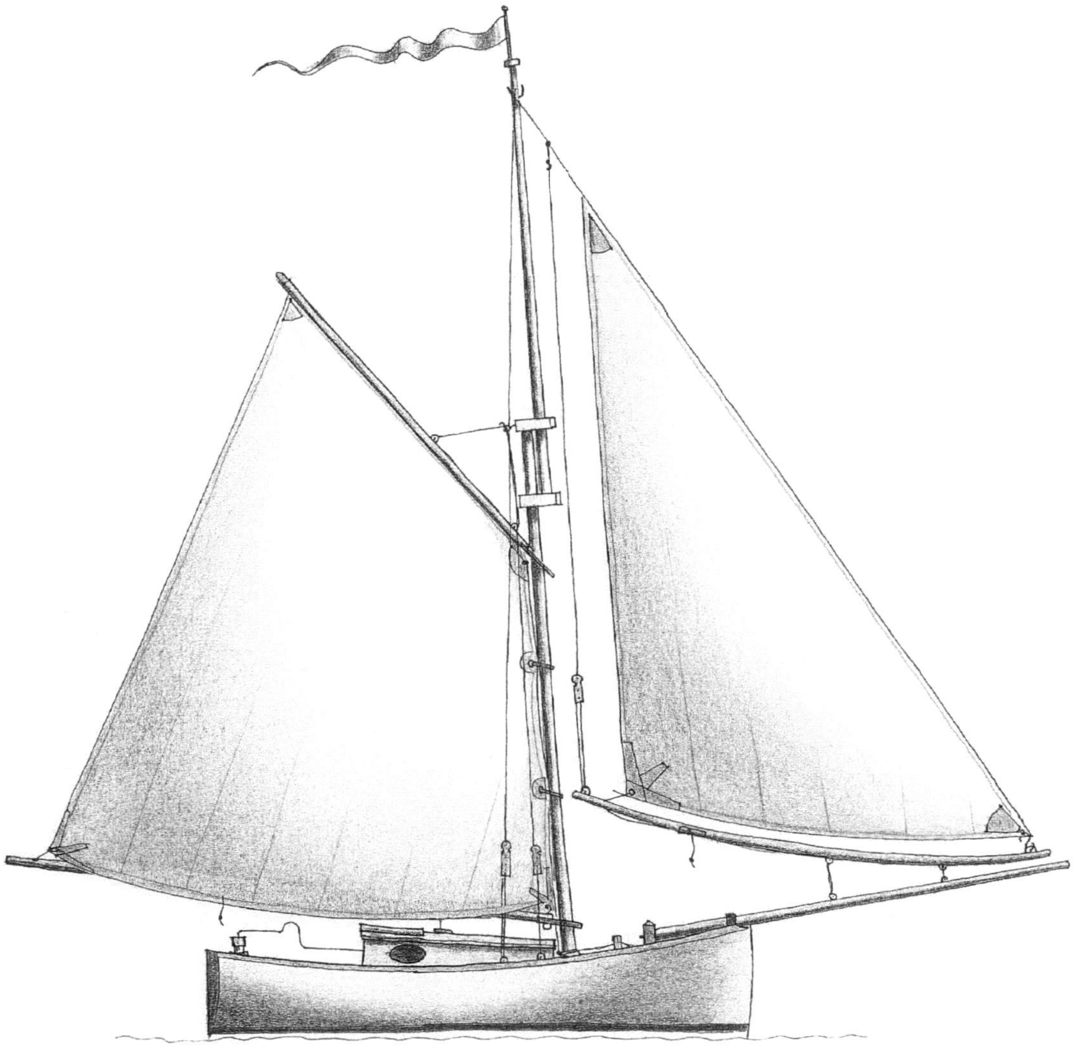

~ Presto ~

Classic footy

LENGTH	322 mm (12" 11/16)
BEAM	100 mm (3" 15/16)
DISPLACEMENT	600 gr. (21 oz)
BALLAST	280 gr. (10 oz)
SAIL AREA	12.3 dm^2 (190 sq in)

Designed by Flavio Faloci

Naval Architect

for

Wooden Boat Magazine

Genova, Italy, May 2011.

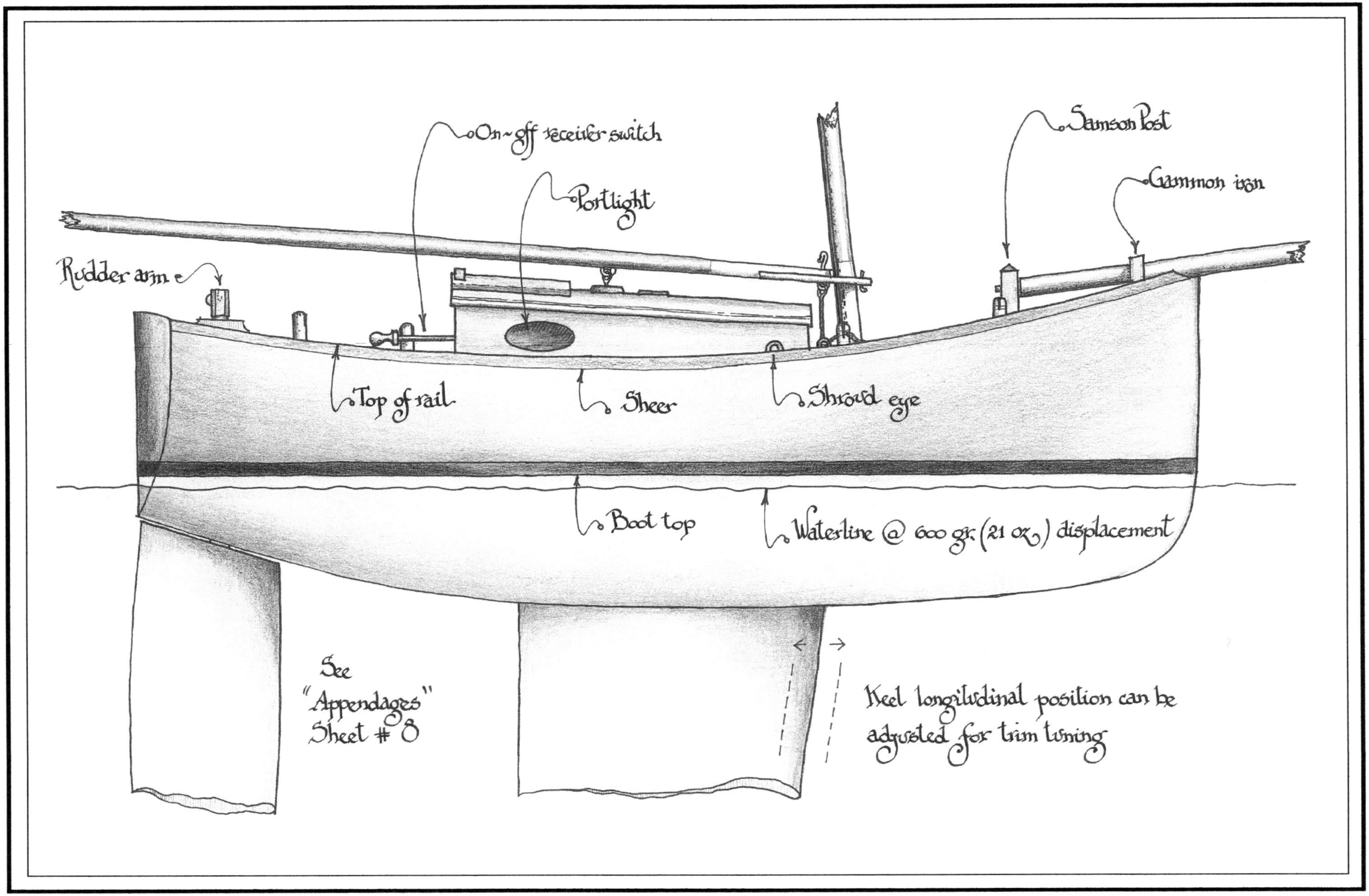

~Presto~ Classic Footy Designed by Flavio Faloci for WoodenBoat ~ Profile ~ Sheet 1

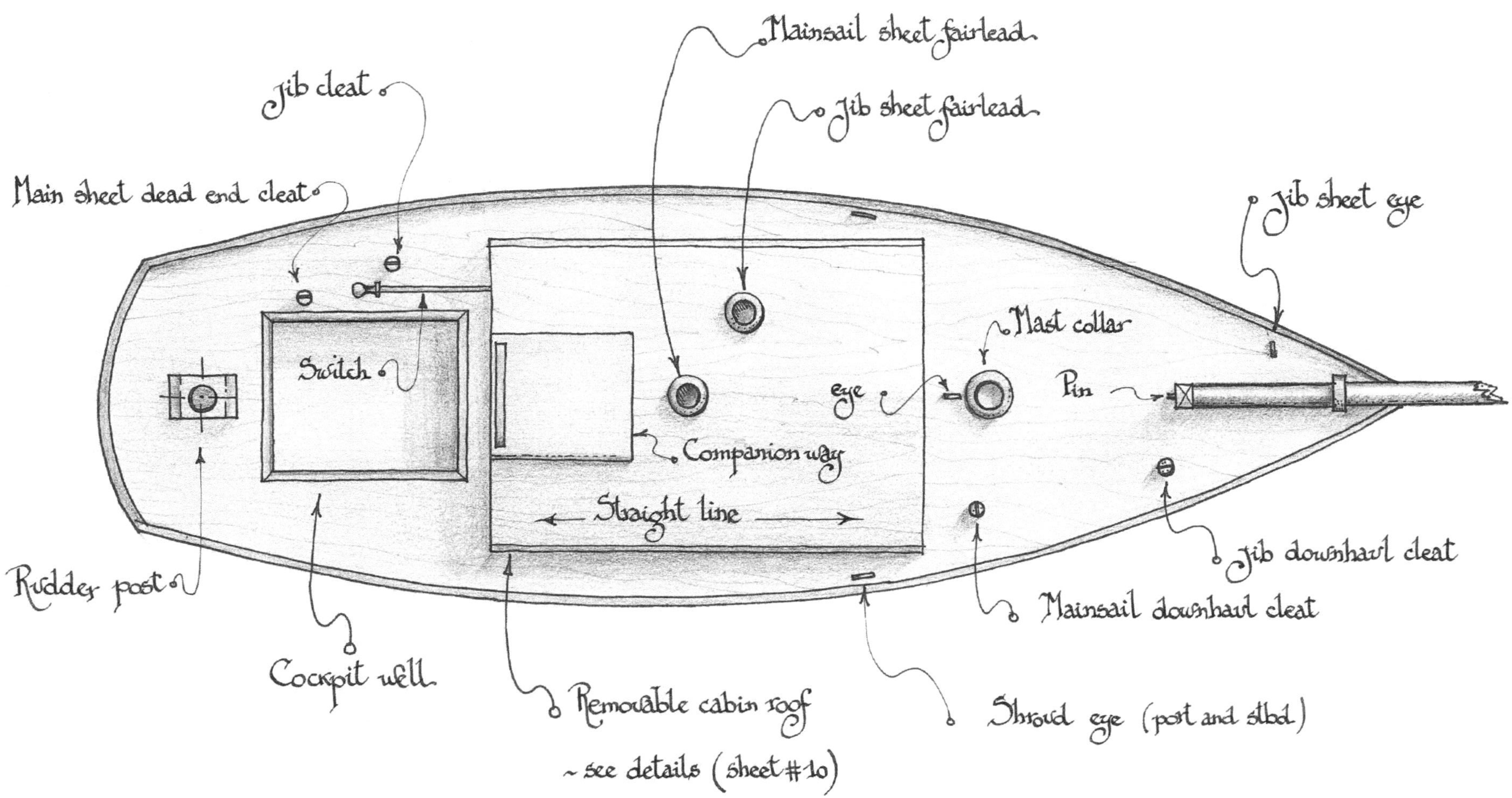

~Presto~ Classic Footy Designed by Flavio Faloci for WoodenBoat ~ Deck plan ~ sheet 2

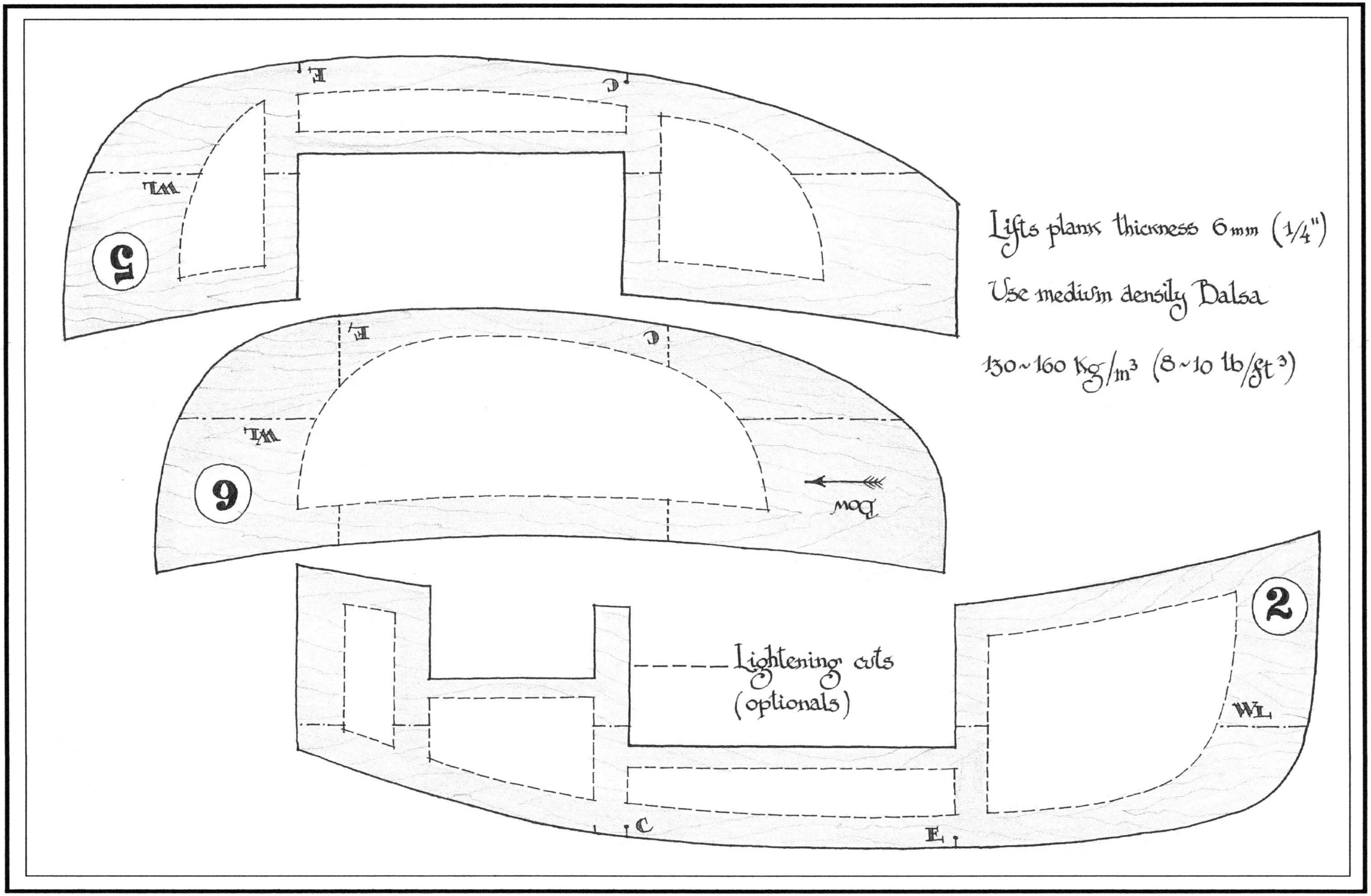

~Presto~Classic Footy Designed by Flavio Faloci for WoodenBoat ~ Templates ~ Sheet 3

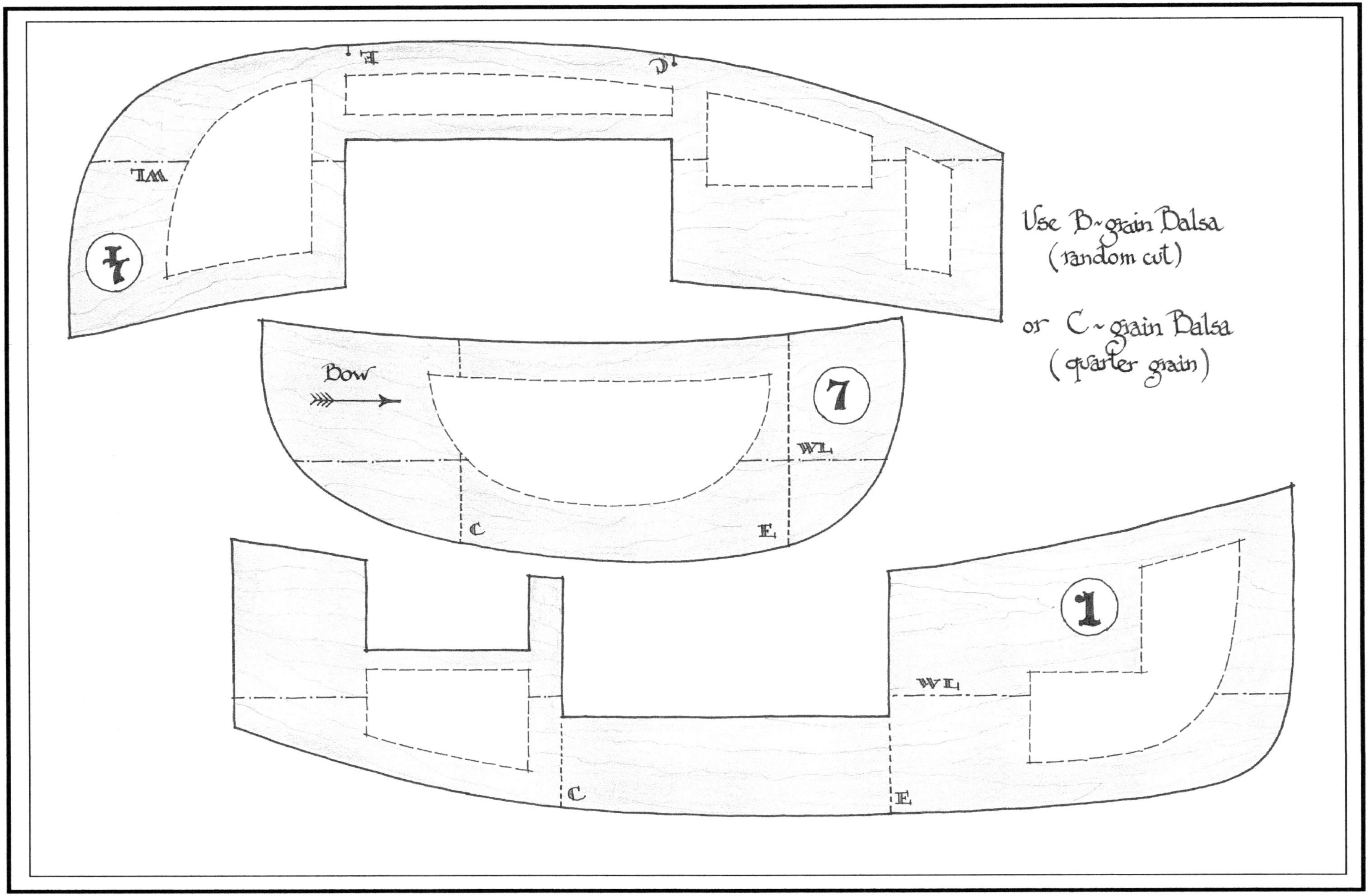

~Presto~Classic Footy Designed by Flavio Faloci for WoodenBoat ~Templates~ Sheet 4

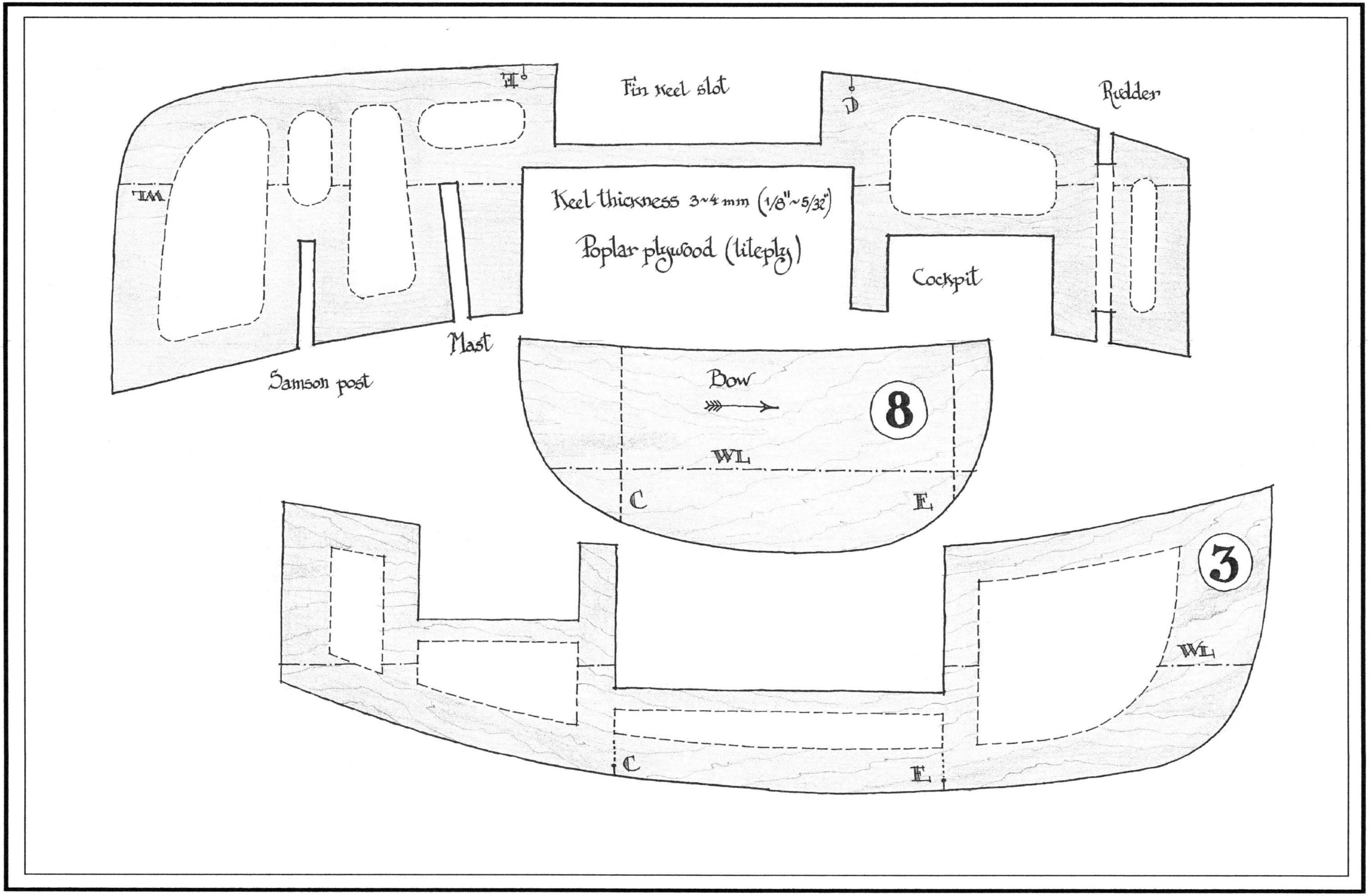

~Presto~Classic Footy Designed by Flavio Faloci for WoodenBoat ~ Templates ~ Sheet 5

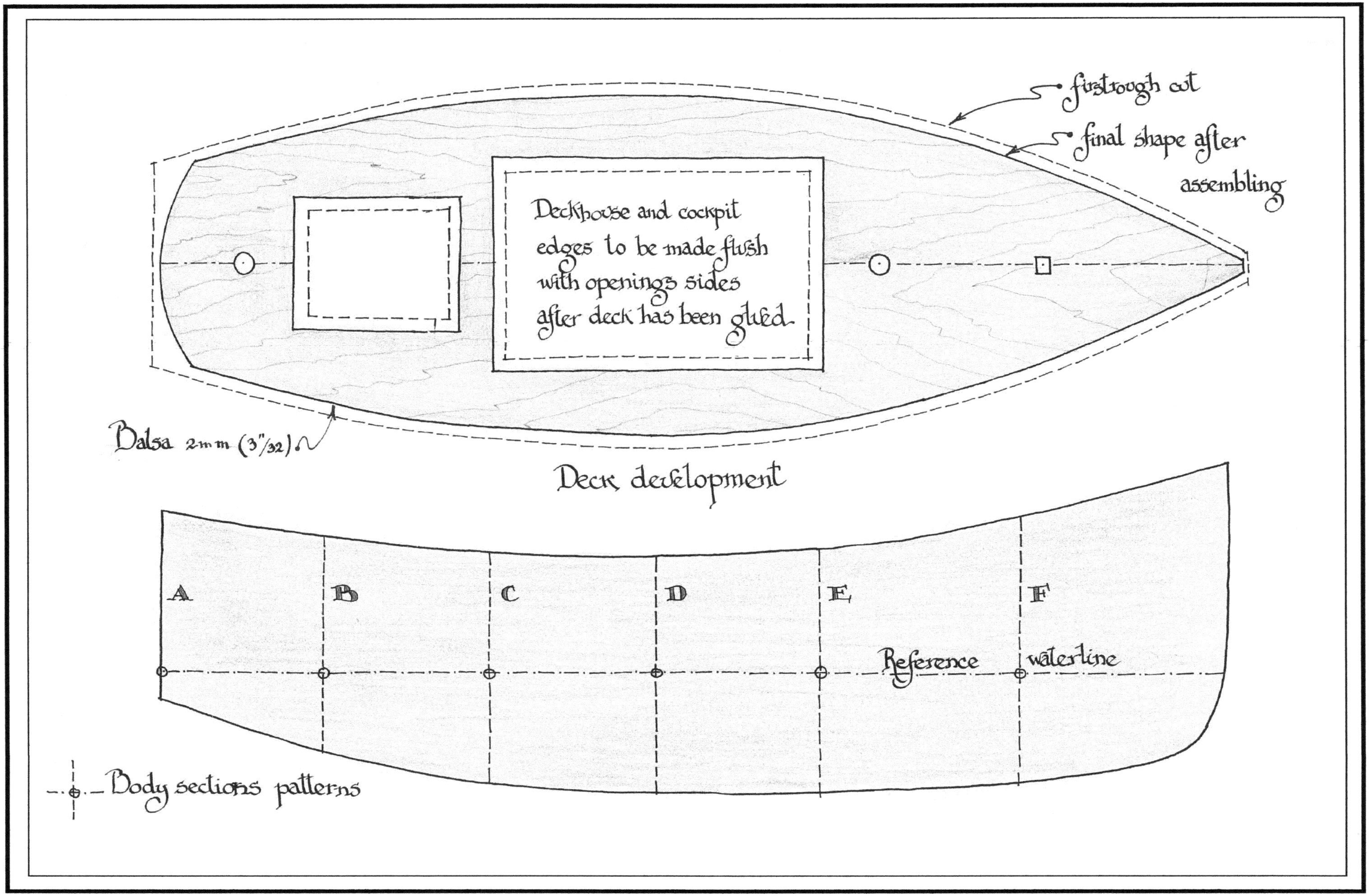

~Presto~Classic Footy Designed by Flavio Faloci for WoodenBoat ~ Templates ~ Sheet 6

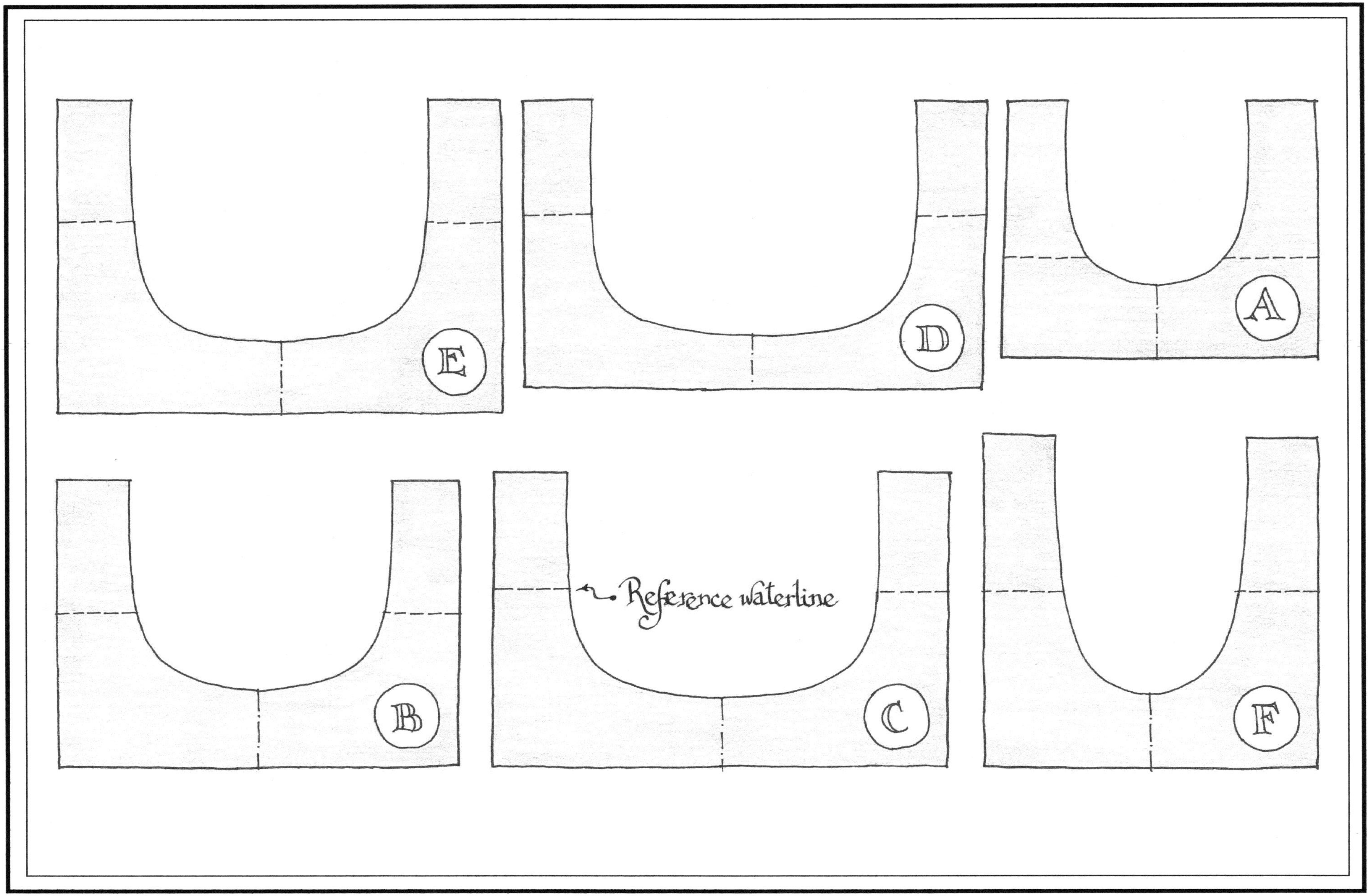

~Presto~Classic Jooty Designed by Flavio Faloci for WoodenBoat ~ Body sections ~ Sheet 7

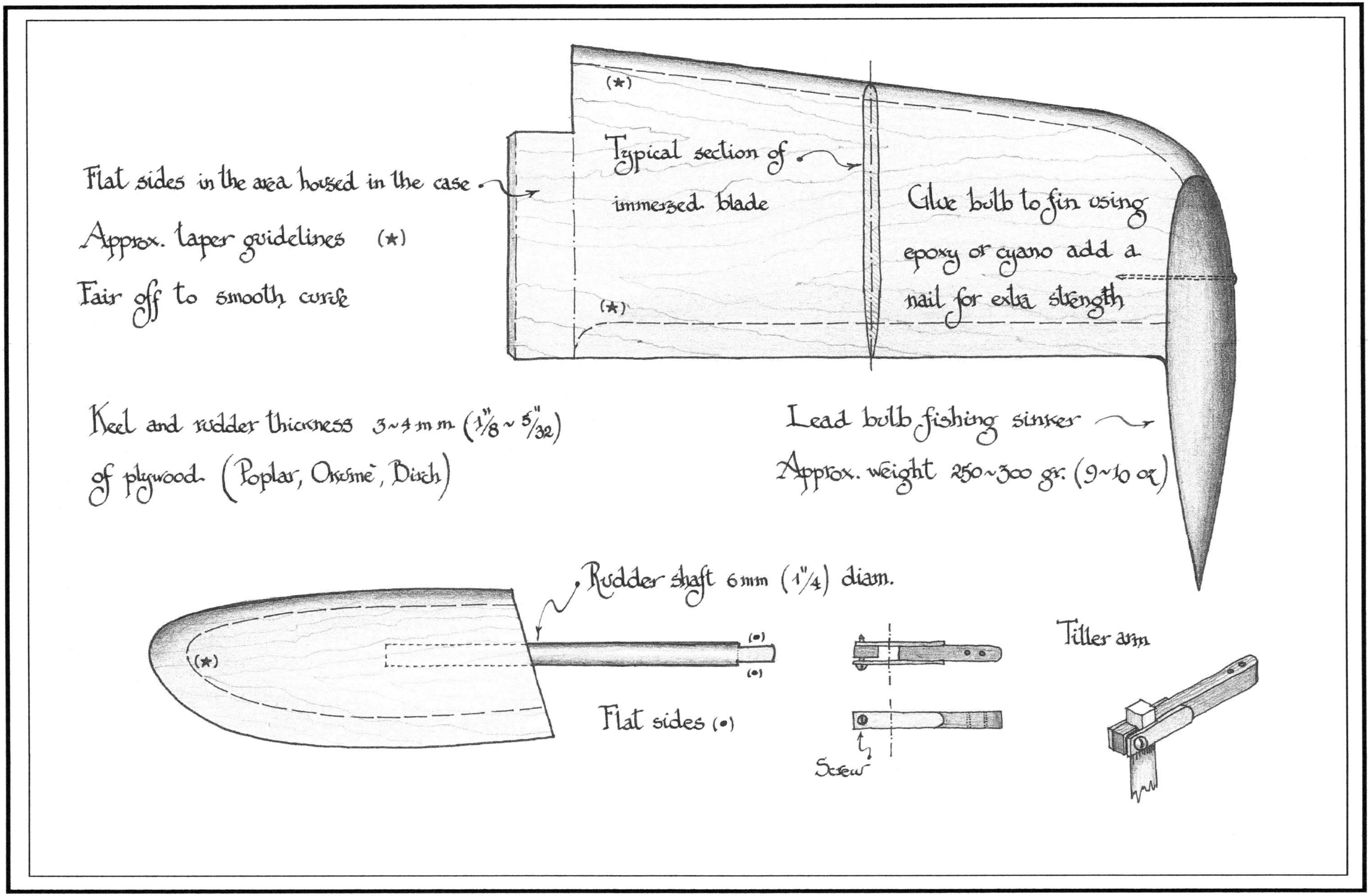

~Presto~ Classic Footy Designed by Flavio Faloci for WoodenBoat ~ Keel and rudder ~ Sheet 8

* Notice: Size of cut outs to be adjusted to fit installed equipment dimensions

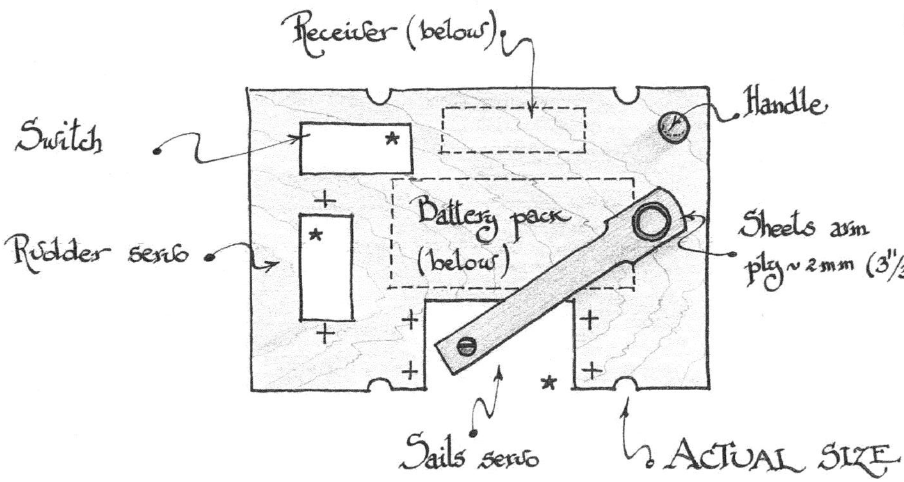

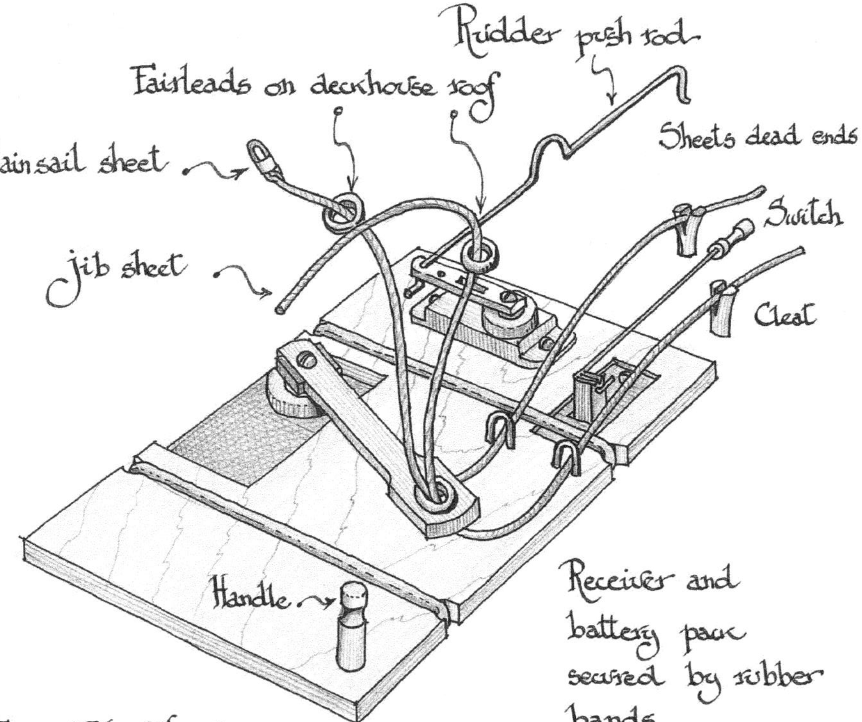

· RC EQUIPMENT ·

Receiver	~ Micro lightweight FM	~ Recommended	: HITEC HFS-05 MS
Sail Servo	~ Torque - 5 kg cm	"	HITEC HS-225 MG
Rudder Servo	~ Torque - 1 kg cm	"	HITEC HS-55
Battery Pack	~ 4 × 1.5 V AAA type	"	Energizer Lithium L 92

~ Presto ~ Classic Footy Designed by Flavio Faloci for WoodenBoat ~ RC mounting plate ~ Sheet 9

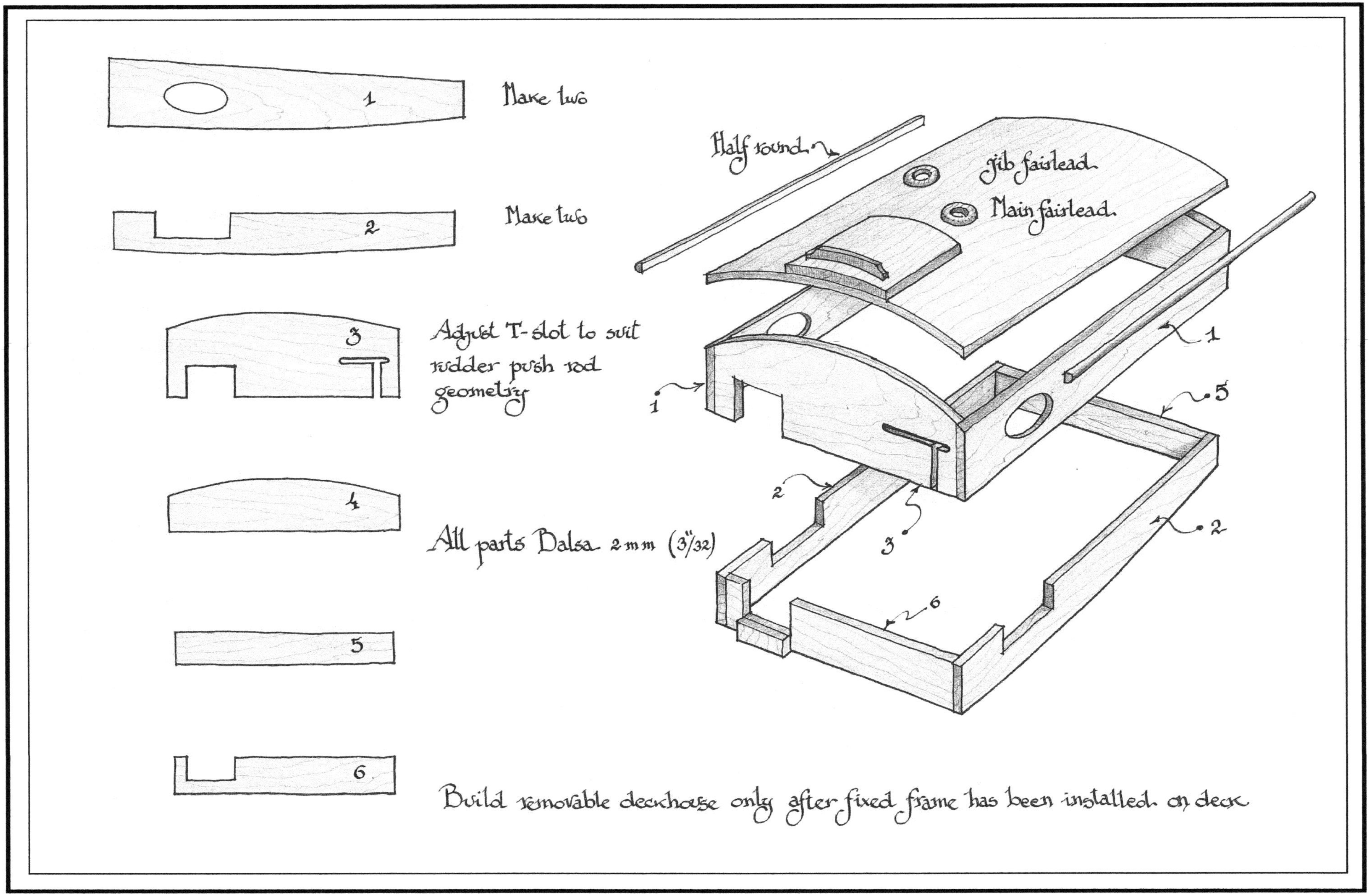

~Presto~Classic Footy Designed by Flavio Faloci for WoodenBoat ~ Deckhouse ~ Sheet 10

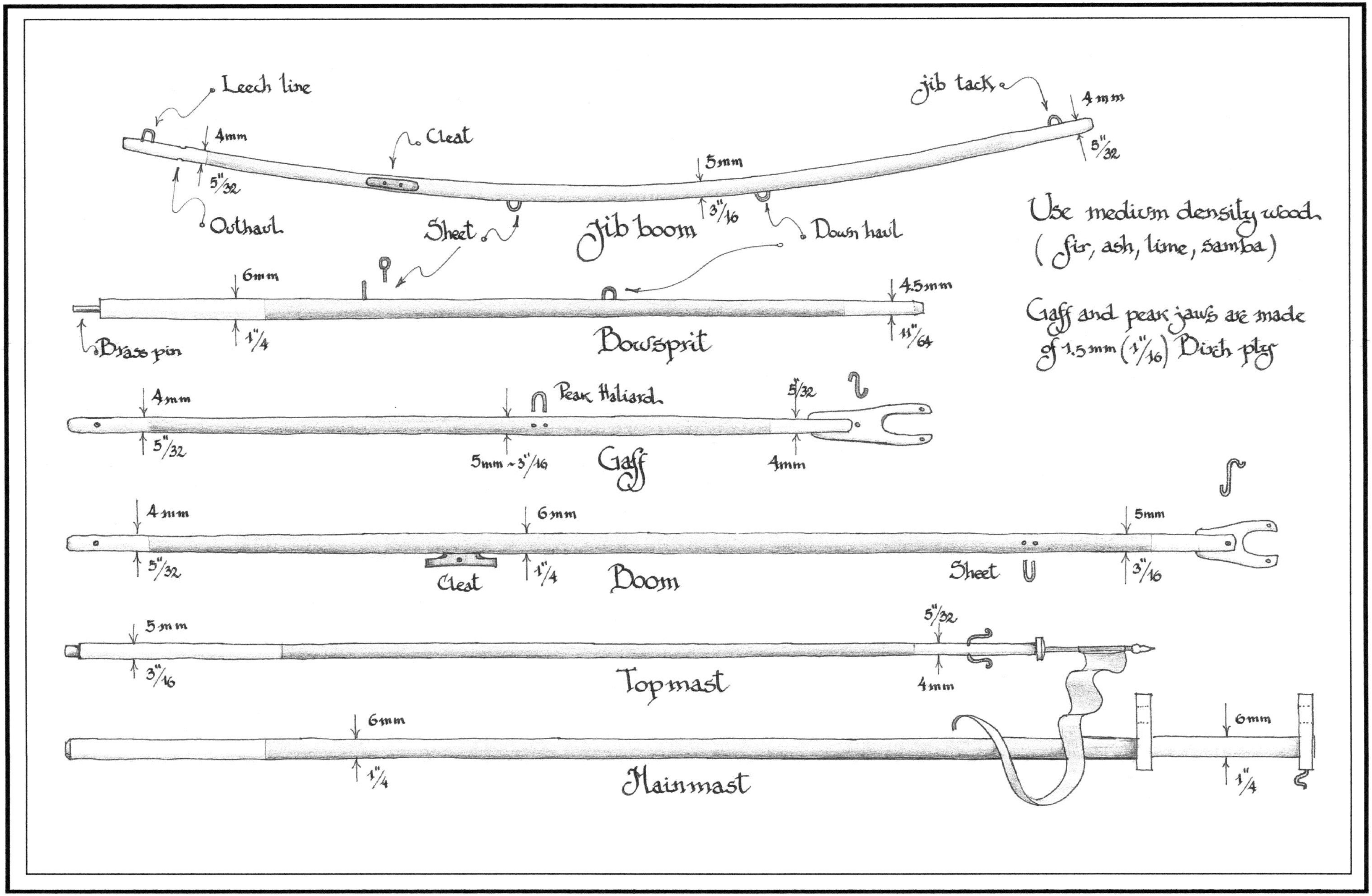

~ Presto ~ Classic Jooly Designed by Flavio Faloci for WoodenBoat ~ Spars ~ Sheet 11

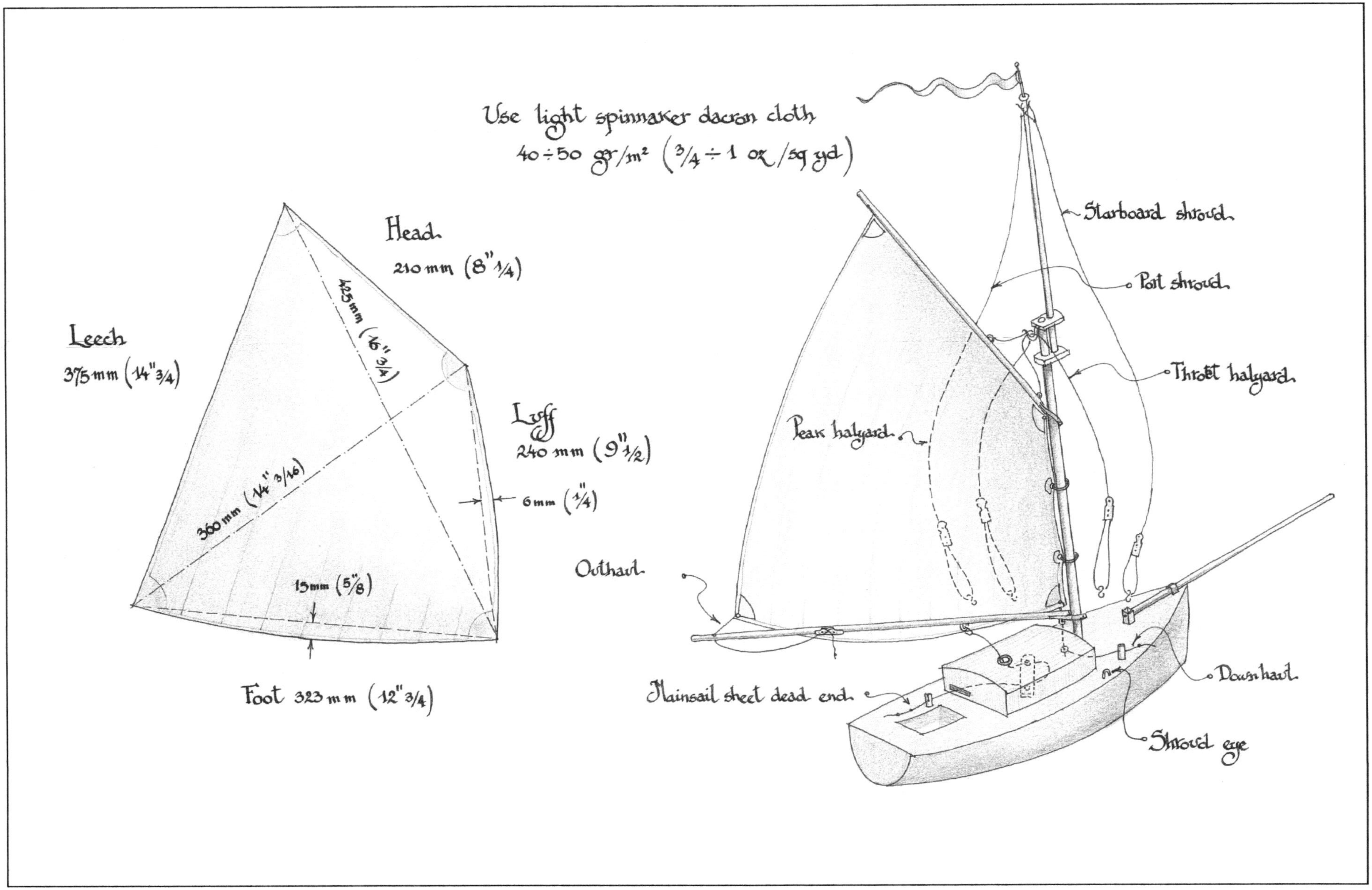

~Presto~Classic Footy Designed by Flavio Faloci for WoodenBoat ~Mainsail rigging~ Sheet 12

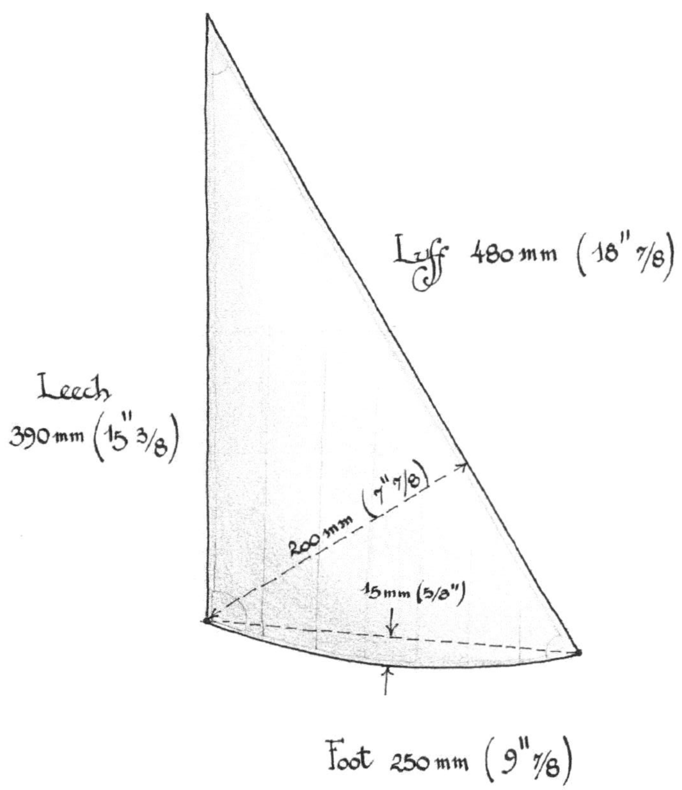

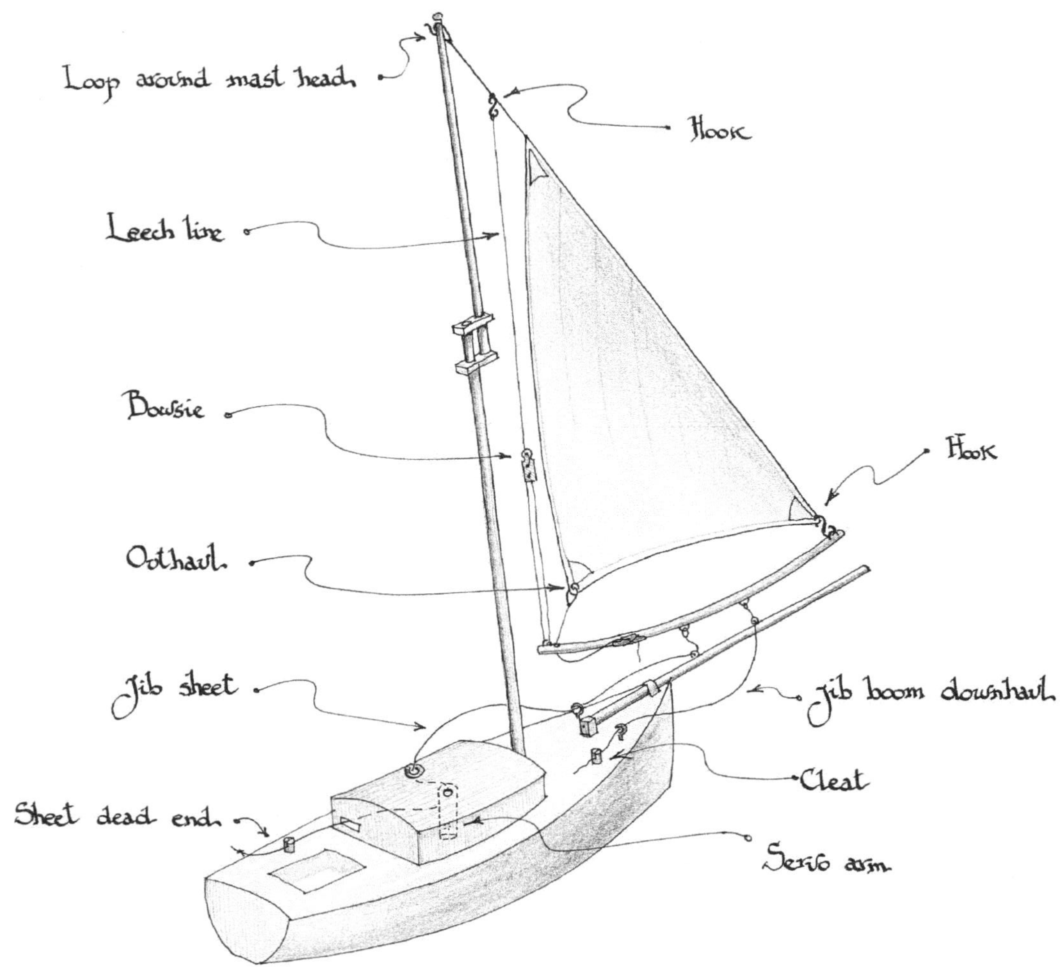

Use light spinnaker dacron cloth: 40÷50 gr/m² (3/4 ÷ 1 oz/sq yd)

~Presto~Classic Footy Designed by Flavio Faloci for WoodenBoat ~ Jib rigging ~ Sheet 13

Templates

1.

Cut-out templates (see sheets #3, 4, 5) using a good pair of scissors, and then glue them onto cardboard (cereal boxes are perfect). Make photocopies of the templates before you cut if you want to keep your plans pages intact.

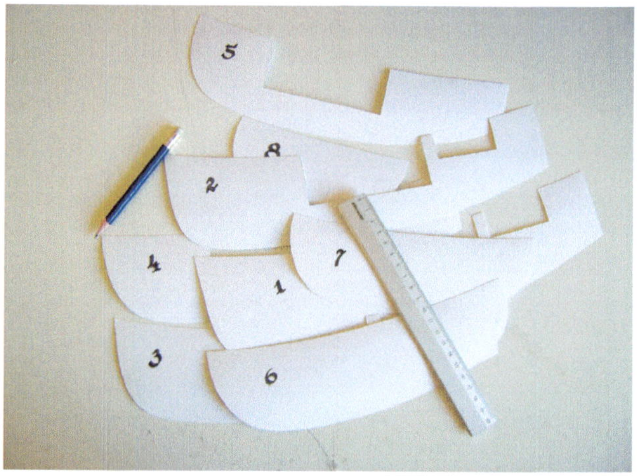

2.

Do the same for transverse body sections See sheet #7.

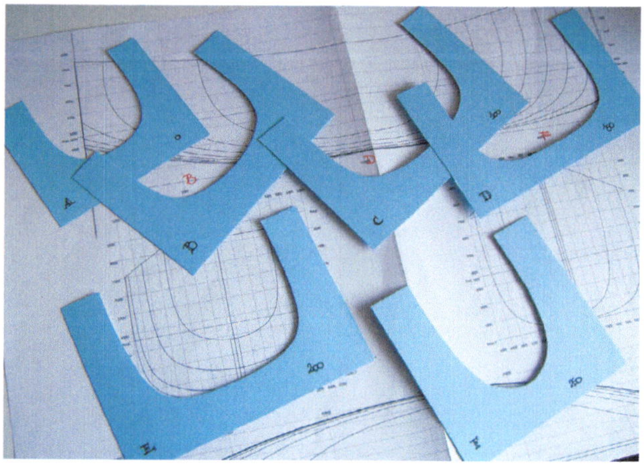

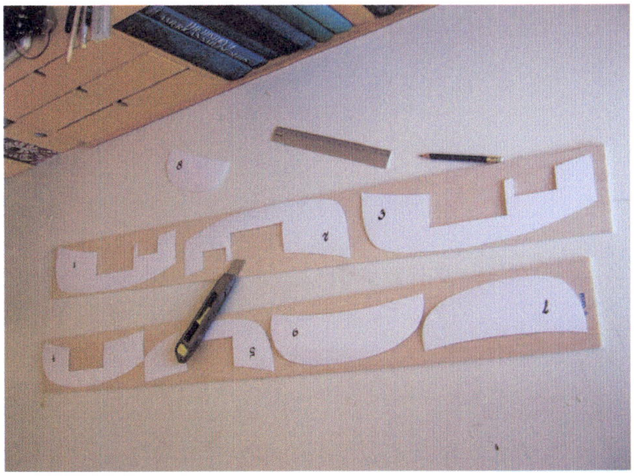

3.

Try to find the best arrangement of templates to make efficient use of your wood. Not more than five standard size balsa planks (1000 mm x 100 mm, or 40"x 4") are necessary. All lifts have same thickness: 6 mm (1/4"). Bread-and-butter building method is very sensitive to wood density, if you are looking to have a decent sailer, your balsa should be medium density quality: not heavier than 130-160 kg/m3 (8-10 lbs/cu ft), B-grain or C-grain. If you are going to varnish your hull, try to use planks with similar texture and color.

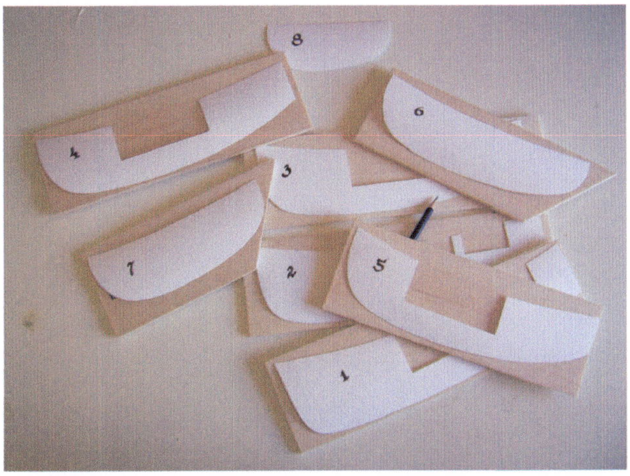

4.

For easier handling break plank length into small parts.

Make two groups (port and starboard) of parts belonging from same planks.

5.

Use a sharp hard pencil to trace pattern shapes on wood.

6.

To avoid confusion, don't forget to mark planks with their reference numbers.

Lifts

7.

Use a sharp blade cutter and a steel ruler to cut straight lines first, such as cockpit contour here.

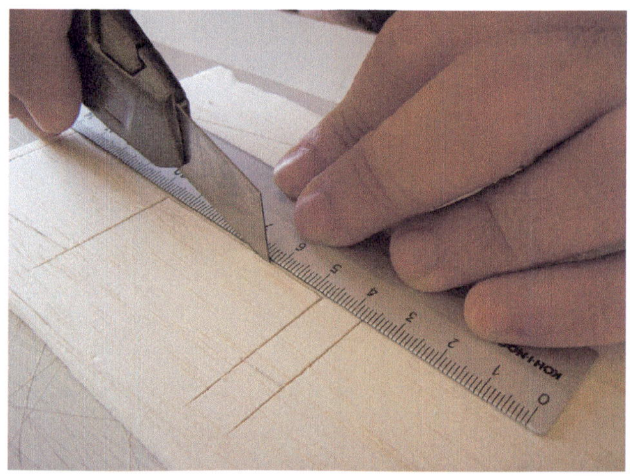

8.

Cut deckline and bottom profiles slightly outside the lines, leaving a bit (2 mm or 1/16") of margin to be removed later.

9.

Carefully remove cutouts from lifts.

10.

If needed (hard bends and/or hard wood) make several tangential straight cuts.

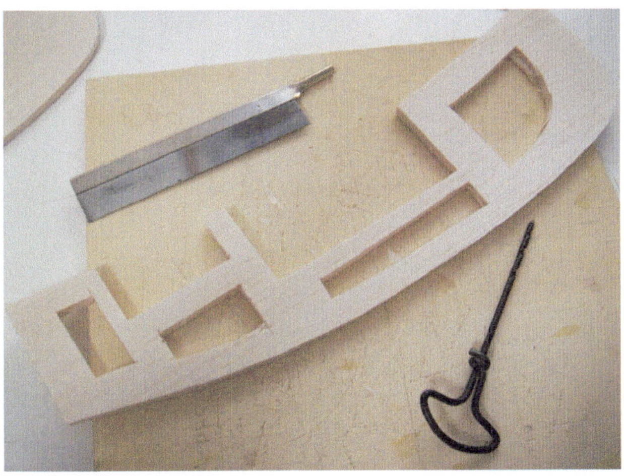

11.

Optional lightening holes can be made to save weight and improve sailing performance.

12.

Pile your 16 planks to check that everything is okay, don't forget that the external lifts (#6, #7, #9) should be oriented with their forward side pointing to the bow!

Keel

13.

Cut plywood keel as a full silhouette. Use, if possible, poplar 3–4 mm (1/8" - 5/32") plywood (also known as liteply).

14.

Mark cutouts lines for samson post, mast, hold, cockpit, and rudder using cardboard templates.

See sheet #5.

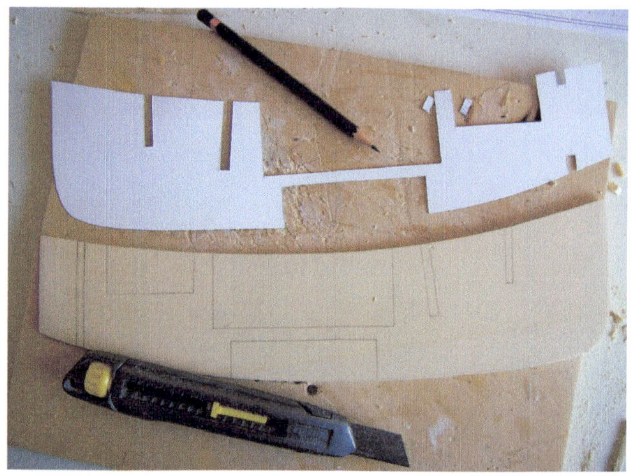

15.

Carve straight lines using a blade cutter: jigsaw cut will be neater and easier during following step.

16.

Make final cuts using a jig or coping saw.

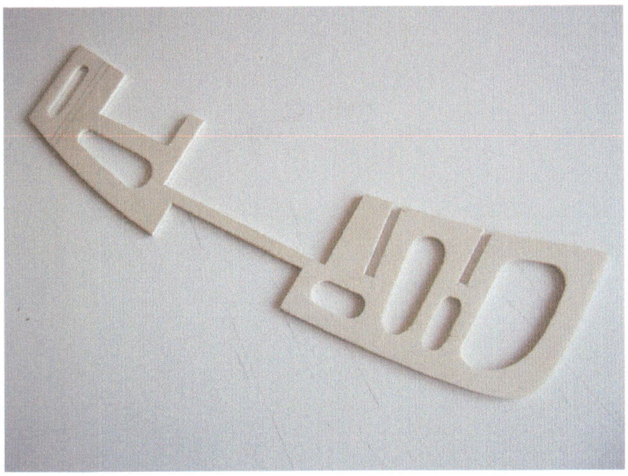

17.

Once again, if you are performance minded, cut lightening holes to save hull weight.

Hull Assembly

18.

Glue balsa lifts to plywood keel, alternating port and starboard planks. Use aliphatic glue.

19.

If you have already built your remote control tray (FCU: Footy control unit, see sheet #9) this is the moment to check how well the electronic stuff fits inside the hold space.

20.

This the very first time that you have something resembling a hull!

Hull Carving

21.

To avoid a huge cloud of sawdust, start the carving process using a knife blade instead of sandpaper block. You'll find chips a bit less intrusive than balsa powder.

Use a brand new sharp blade, and move it with gentle strokes from midship to extremities (bow and stern) following the wood grain.

22.

This the most important step during model building so take your time, relax, listen music and try to work under direct sunlight.

To avoid a complete failure, remove small chips of wood at each stroke.

23.

You will be impressed by the huge amount of chips which can be produced by so small a boat!

24.

As the boat's shape begins to emerge, check sections using transverse body templates.

25.

Start with coarse grade sandpaper, moving to smoother grades during final touch up.

Deck

26.

Cut deck plank, (2 mm – 3/32" balsa) slightly oversized, glue it to hull, holding parts in place by pins.

Don't forget pilot holes for mast, samson post and rudderstock.

(Photo shows the first prototype of *Presto*, without cockpit well.)

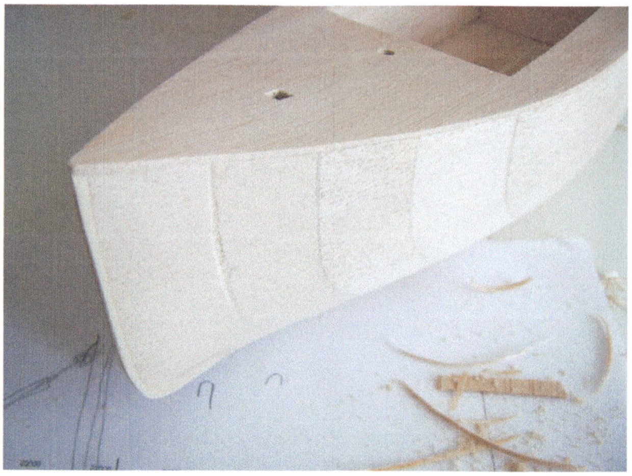

27.

Trim deck edge flush with topsides.

28.

Add toe rail, a square section of balsa wood 2 mm x 2 mm (3/32” x 3/32”).

29.

Add half-round trim along cockpit edge.

30.

If you wish you can now give first the coat of thinned varnish.

Stern Transom

31.

Presto has been designed as a "diagonal" Footy, and a rounded transom has been conceived to take advantage of maximum hull length within standard rulebox.

If you are not interested in having your model in compliance to international Footy rules, you can build a flat transom without affecting sailing performance. It would speed-up the building process.

32.

Trace rounded deck profile, and make vertical cuts to remove stern corners.

33.

If you haven't your own rulebox, verify how deck contour fits within a 152 x 305 mm (6" x 12") rectangle drawn on a sheet of paper.

34.

Add aft deck toerail, and refine transom shape using sandpaper.

35.

To avoid potential damages or dents to stern edge, add a thin sheet of birch ply, or other hardwood. Cut it slightly oversized, and trim stern sheating flush with hull sides. Add a second coat of varnish.

Deckhouse

36.

Glue fixed inner parts of deckhouse to deck.

See sheet #10.

37.

Hold together parts of removable deckhouse cover with pins instead of glue!

38.

Test the fixed hatch for fit on the hull, and adjust as necessary, using sandpaper until you get a snug fit.

39.

After sides have been stitched together, add the roof.

40.

Trim roof flush with sides and add two half-round strips along edges.

41.

Add a fake companionway and glue (from the inside) two clear plastic sheets to close portlights.

42.

Add two wooden rings as mainsail and jib sheets fairleads (plastic beads are also okay). Add a third coat of varnish.

Labels

43.

Your model is almost half way built, so you can now relax with a simpler job session.

44.

Add a small builder plate inside cockpit well. It could be useful to recall when you built *Presto,* many years from now.

45.

Footy Class Rules: "The hull registration number shall be clearly and legibly marked in an easily visible location either inside or outside on a non-removable part of the hull by any of the following means: painting on, engraving in, moulding."

46.

Make tests of your favorite nameplate style on scrap pieces of hardwood.

47.

Add nameplate to stern using glue and a pair of decorative small brass nails, peened brass rod, or just glue.

48.

If you wish you can even add small labels to remember correct on/off position of switch, as well identify deadends of sail sheets. Add a fourth coat of varnish.

Rudder

49.

Cut rudder blade from a piece of
4 - 5 mm (5/32" - 3/16") poplar plywood.

See sheet #8.

50.

If you like you can use also birch plywood. It's harder, heavier, and smoother.

51.

File and sand the blade to something resembling a foil (round nose and sharp tail), and cut a slot for rudderstock.

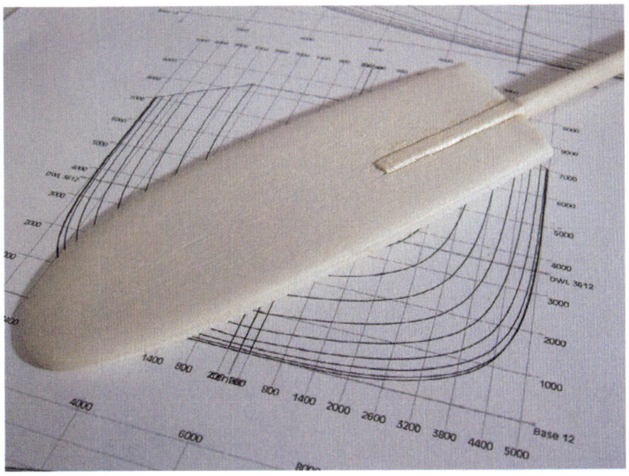

52.

Glue wooden stock to the blade and trim it flush with rudder sides.

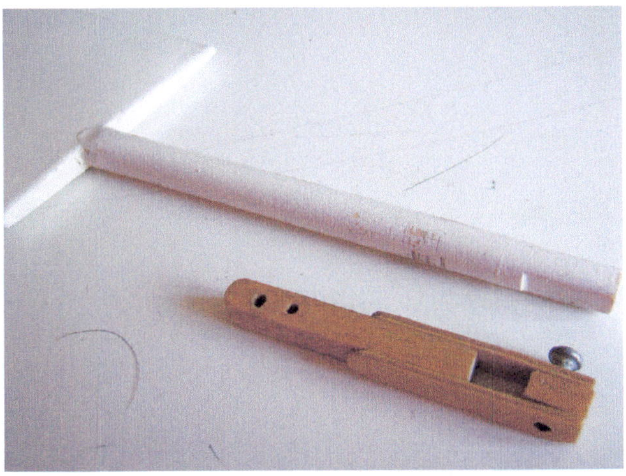

53.

Build tiller arm, and file upper end of rudderstock squared to fit it.

54.

Tiller arm shall be on starboard side (to right side!) to be linked by a push rod to its servo.

Brass pushrod has a U-shaped bend to fine-tune its length for better rudder centering.

55.

Make your own experiments, testing different shapes and sizes of rudder blade.

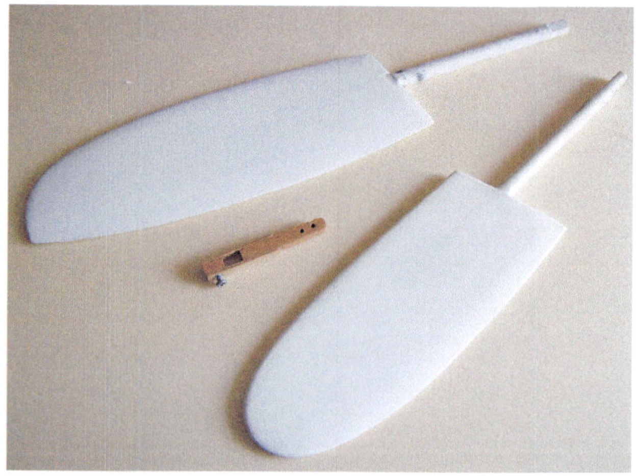

56.

Don't forget the rudder upper end shall match the hull bottom slope, in order to have a minimum gap between blade and hull.

57.

I prefer to give to the hull not less than 6-7 coats of varnish, but if you are in hurry you can now give first coat of paint to hull bottom and to the rudder.

58.

Mark waterline using adhesive tape, and give first coat of paint. I like white bottoms.

Fin Keel

59.

Use a fishing sinker (250-300 gr/9-10 oz) as a ballast bulb.

See sheet #8.

60.

Remove forward end.

61.

Make nose round, and file it to something streamlined.

Wear gloves and a dust mask as lead is poisonous! It is especially dangerous for small children and pregnant women. Inhalation or ingestion of lead or lead dust can cause lead poisoning. Wash hands and change clothes before doing anything else. Clean-up area with disposable wipes, then bag the wipes. Paint keel bulb right away, for more protection.

62.

Sand lead surface as smooth as possible using sandpaper first, and emerypaper for final touch. Two different ballast sizes are shown here.

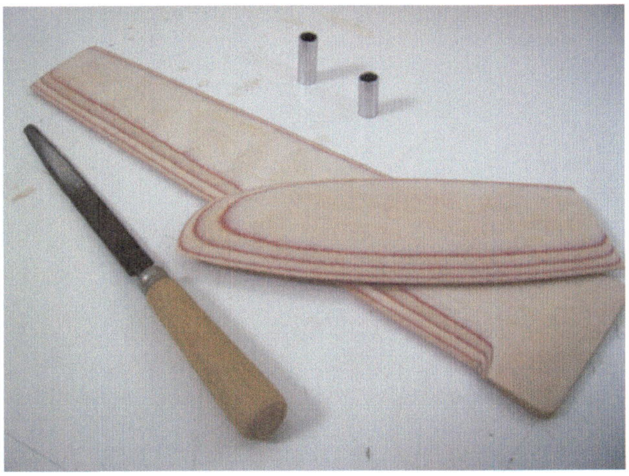

63.

Cut fin from plywood (birch in this photo) and carefully file a round leading edge and a sharp trailing edge.

64.

Adjust fin lower end to fit bulb contour, and glue them together using epoxy or cyano.

If you wish, you can glue the keel (forever...) inside the hull slot, but I prefer to keep it in place only by friction, adjusting keel thickness and case width.

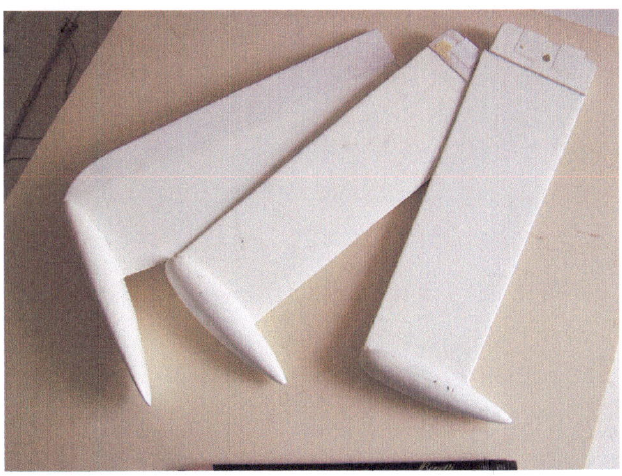

65.

If you use a friction fit for the keel, you have plenty of options. You can test different weights, sizes and shapes to suit various weather conditions.

66.

Give a second coat of paint to hull bottom and to appendages.

Spars

67.

Cut dowels (or square stock) to size, slighty longer than needed, to make spars: lower mast, topmast, boom, gaff, bowsprit.

See sheet #11.

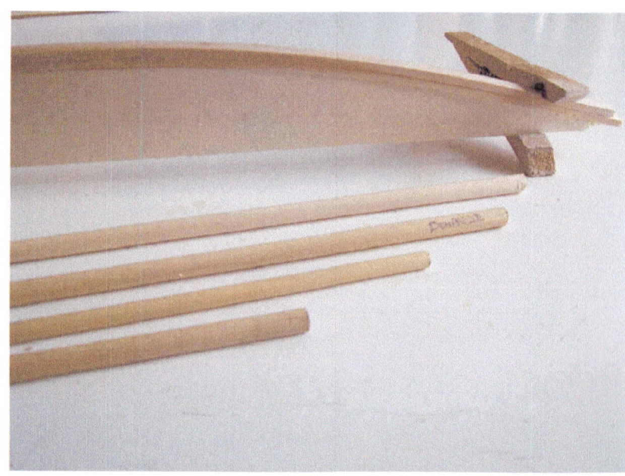

68.

Glue thin strips of wood on a mold to laminate a curved jib boom. Create the mold yourself based on the curve of the plans drawing.

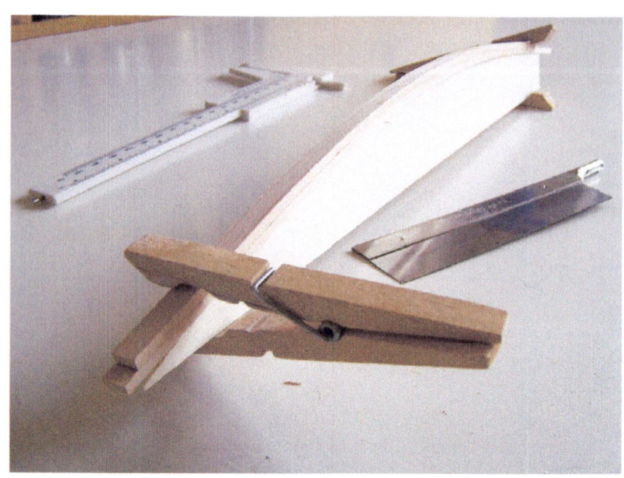

69.

Use a small planer to taper spar ends. If you use square stock (Sitka spruce is especially nice) make a centerline down the length to keep symetrical. Cut to the lines, then trim the edges of the four-sided wood with a file, rasp or sandpaper block, to form an eight-sided piece. Sand the sharp edges until the spar is round. Use increasingly fine sheets of sandpaper.

70.

Use a blade knife to make jib boom eight sided, and coarse sandpaper to make it round and tapered.

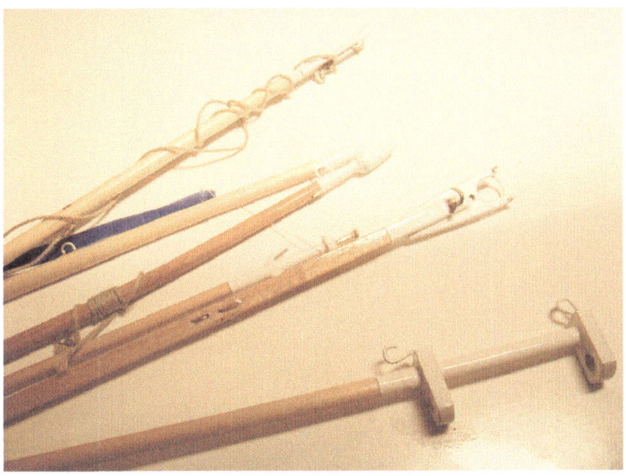

71.

There are not less than six sticks to build. Seven if you like topsails.

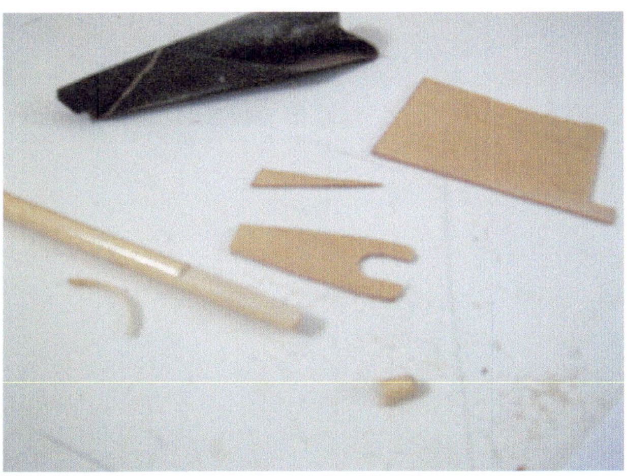

72.

Build gaff and boom jaws using thin birch plywood, and glue them to the spar ends.

73.

Boom forward end as finished. Note mainsail sheet, and boom downhaul.

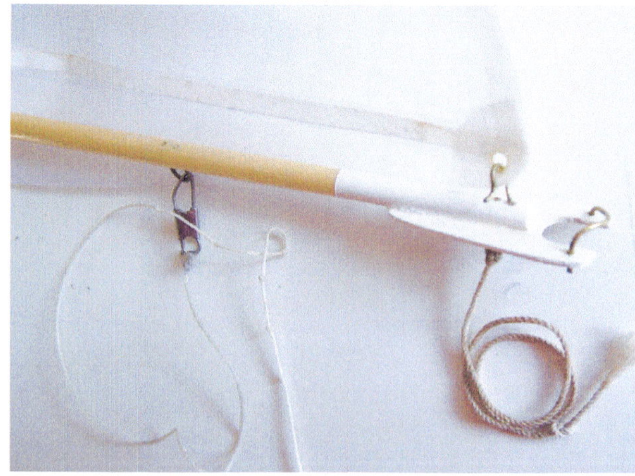

74.

Gaff jaws as finished. Note throat halyard.

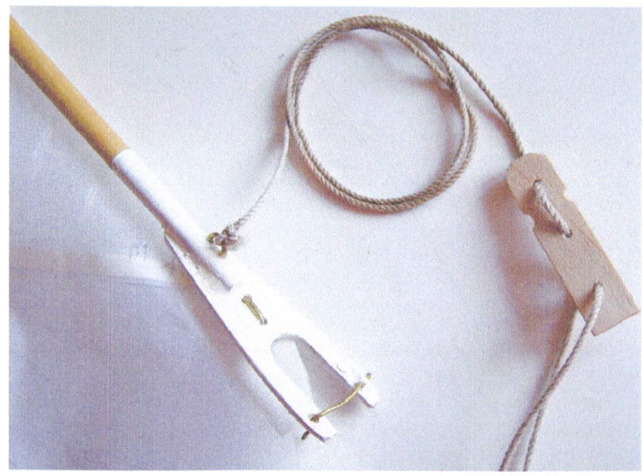

75.

Mainmast head fittings.

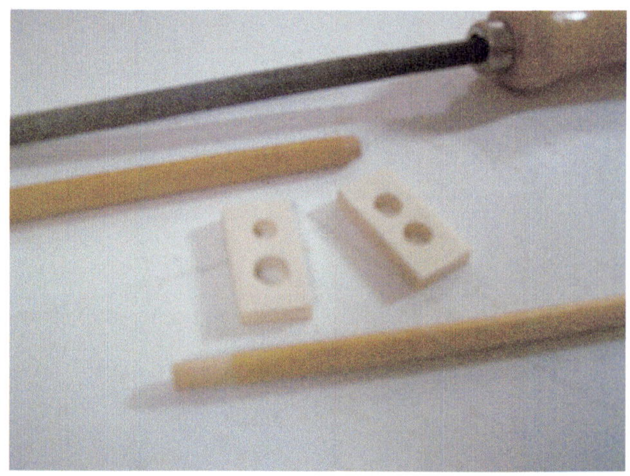

76.

Mast and topmast. Note tapering of lower side of topmast.

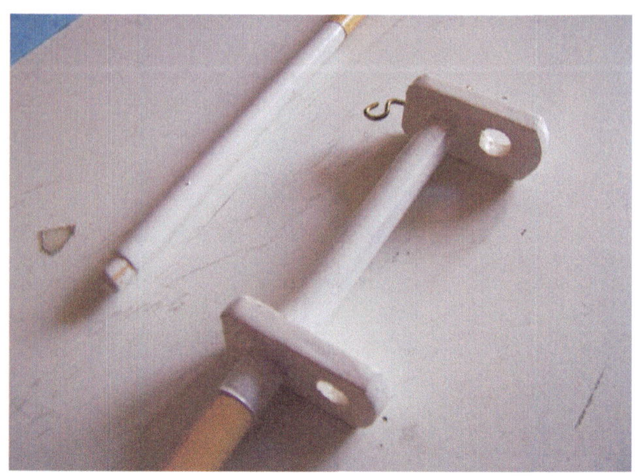

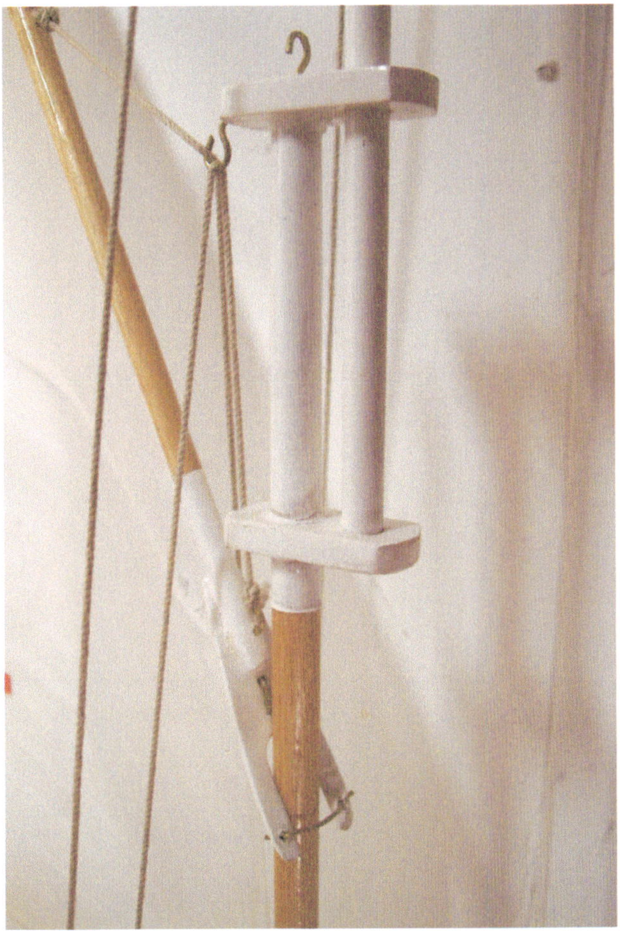

77.

As finished.

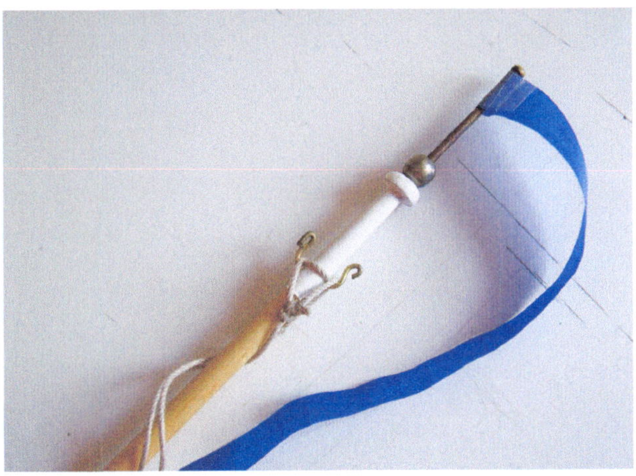

78.

Topmast head.

79.

Cleat on mainsail boom, for outhaul line.

Give a couple of coats of varnish to spars, and then paint white ends as final touch.

Give a final coat of paint to hull bottom.

Deck Fittings

80.

Use a square sided hardwood stick to build the samson post, drill the small hole before gluing it in place.

See sheet #2 for deck outfitting details.

81.

Insert a small brass pin into rear end of bowsprit to connect it to the samson post. The small brass eye on the left is the jib sheet fairlead.

82.

Add bitts for jib and mainsail downhauls, and jib and main sheets deadends. I use bamboo chop-sticks I save from dining out.

Add chainplates made using U-shaped brass wire. The bowsprit gammon iron is made by a thin strip of brass, or brass rod. Hold these fittings in place with cyano (Super/Crazy) glue.

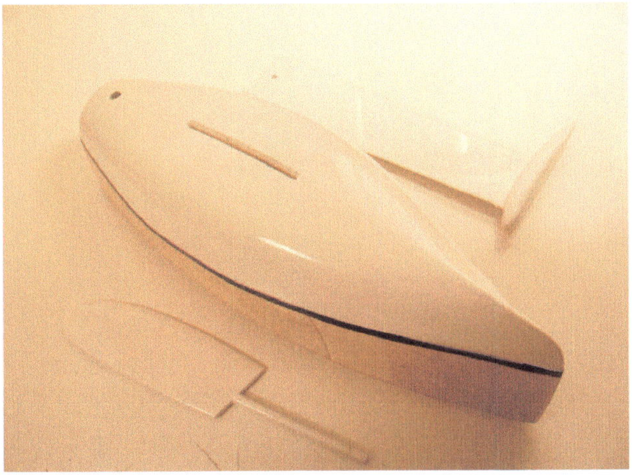

83.

Add a black boot top line, made by using a strip of plastic adhesive paper.

Sails

84.

Make sails using light spinnaker cloth: 40-50 gr/m² (3/4 - 1 oz/sq yd).

See sheets #12, #13 for sail dimension details.

85.

If you are a skilled model sailmaker, make a paneled sail to achieve a more aerodynamic sail shape. In this case I used three panels on each sail. Note red wool telltales for racing sail trimming.

86.

Make sail registration numbers using plastic adhesive paper, using a classic nice style. Please avoid Arial or other unpleasant fonts.

87.

Make birch wood bowsies (also called bowsers) for shrouds and halyard tensioning.

See sheets #12, #13 for rigging details.

88.

Enjoy yourself with a old fashioned topsail if you are sailing in light airs.

89.

Build a reduced-sized storm rig for winter sailing in bad weather.

FCU - Footy Control Unit

90.

A removable RC tray is, in my opinion, the only way to install electronic "objects" without incurring psychiatric diseases. Don't underestimate the need of powerful sail servos (use of "metal gear" versions is strongly recommended). Footy class rules have been modified, so use of AA batteries is no longer mandatory, and smaller/lighter options are now allowed. I use (non-rechargeable) AAA batteries.

See sheet #9.

91.

FCU plank shown here is balsa. Harder strips of wood have been added to have "meat" for screws.

92.

Receiver and battery pack are held in place using rubber bands.

On - off switch is installed between small balsa blocks (FCU shown here as seen from below).

93.

Custom made sail sheet arm has been built using birch plywood.

A metal ring has been inserted, to reduce friction, as fairlead for sail sheets.

94.

Switch button has been drilled, and a brass push-rod has been installed into this hole to activate the receiver without removing deckhouse roof. More than one hour has been spent (wasted?) to fashion the micro wooden handle.

95.

FCU can be removed for battery replenishment or repairs. Wooden pin on forward port corner has been added to be used as a handle.

96.

This a stronger and heavier plywood version of Presto's FCU.

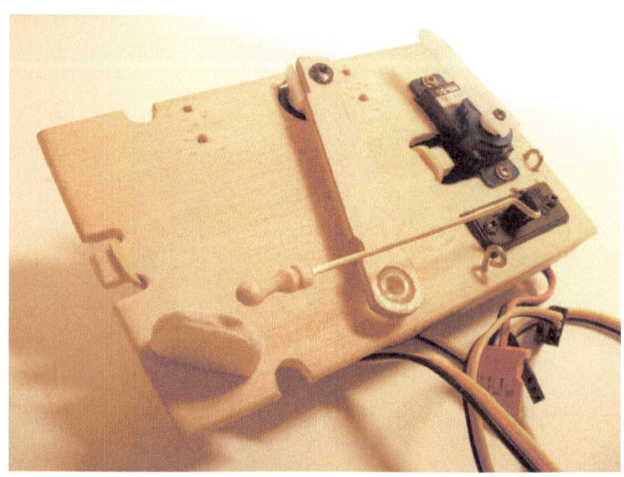

Stands

97.

A proper wooden stand is a very useful object during final building steps, as well during early steps.

98.

This foldable version is simple and practical, and can be used as a shore base during sailing activity.

99.

This alternative is a more artistic version, not so stable, to display your model.

More Design Ideas

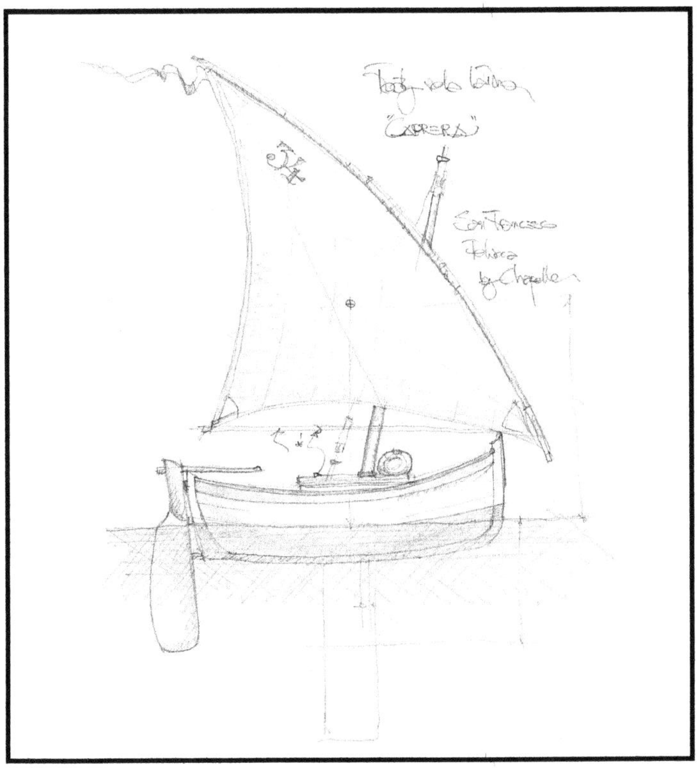

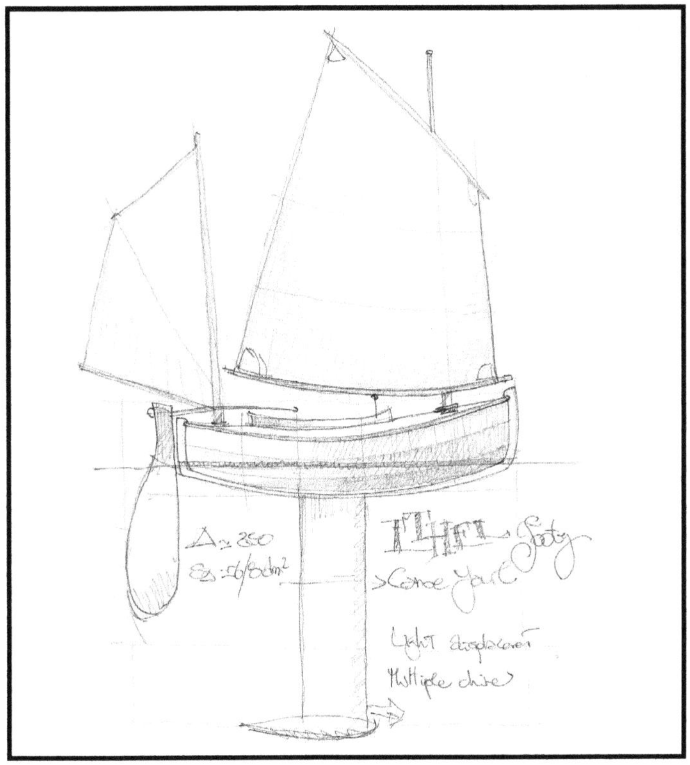

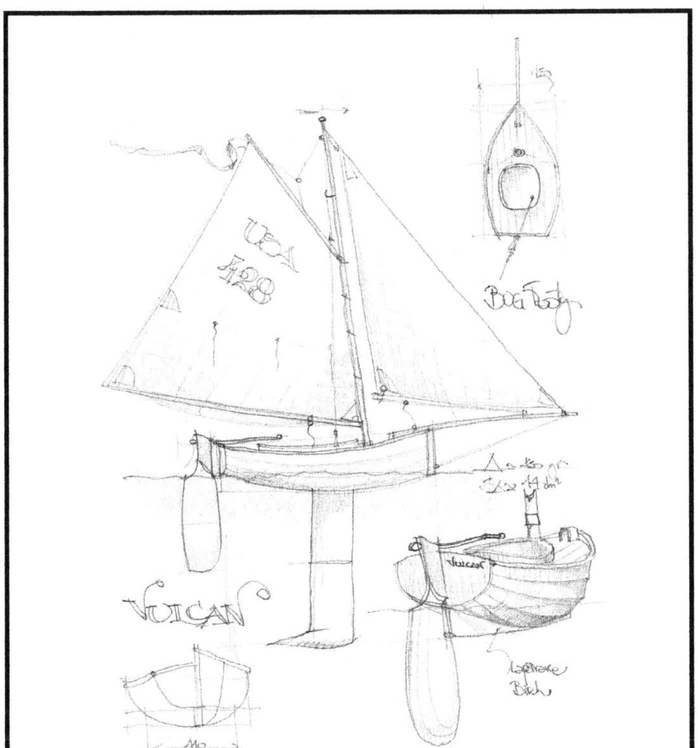

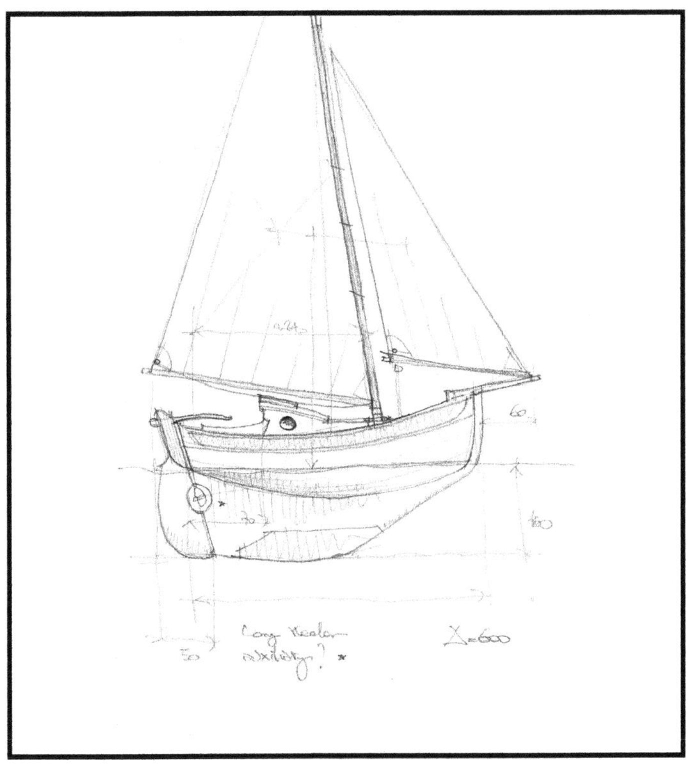